In *The Future is Bivocational,* Andrew Hamilton casts a compelling vision for bivocational mission and ministry. He not only provides a strong biblical and missiological rationale for bivocational leadership, but he also shares practical insight on the benefits and challenges of being bivocational. I *really* love this book. I will recommend it often to pastors and church planters.

Brad Brisco
Director of Bivocational Church Planting for the North American Mission Board and author of 'Missional Essentials' and 'Next Door as It Is in Heaven'

Andrew is an experienced and insightful bivocational pastor. He has written a challenging book, calling the church to reconsider its bivocational roots and to explore this dimension as the means to a healthy and vibrant missional future. The Future is Bivocational ought to be read and taken seriously by all pastors who seek effective missional engagement and connection with the world around them.

Alan Hirsch
Founding Director of Forge Mission Training Network

This book is the most important book I've read on ministry in the last decade. Bivocational ministry is not just a fad. This form of ministry has deep roots in the church's history and is the most common form of ministry in World Christianity. Bivocational ministry is revolutionising our current practices of ministry. Andrew Hamilton writes out of deep conviction and practical experience. This book shows us how to navigate the challenges and opportunities of the bivocational life. The future is bivocational. Every church leader should read this book. Andrew Hamilton's book should be on the reading list of all ministry teams and in every ministry training program.

Graham Joseph Hill
Author of "Holding Up Half the Sky" and State Leader for Baptist Mission Australia WA

This is an exceptionally helpful book on a topic of great relevance. Relatable stories merge seamlessly with significant theological insights to build a persuasive case that opting for a bivocational ministry is not a second best choice when finance is absent, but one which opens doors to ministry in life serving and authentic ways. Andrew Hamilton is a clear and practical thinker, a seasoned practitioner who supplements his experience with wide reading, and an outstanding missiologist. This book also demonstrates that he is an excellent writer. It has deepened my thinking. The future is indeed bivocational, and that is to be celebrated.

Dr Brian Harris
Director, AVENIR Leadership Institute; former Principal, Vose Seminary, Perth.

This is not a book of mere theories. Having worked alongside Andrew for over fourteen years I have seen the principles written here lived out first hand by the author. A timely book for anyone considering entering paid ministry or for those reassessing their careers. The down to earth approach is easy to follow and thoroughly authentic. Do yourself a favour and read it.

Ryan Cristonsen
Pastoral Team Leader Yanchep Community Church

Andrew has written a work of great quality delivering powerful insights on living for Jesus in our world. Born out of reflecting deeply on a life spent walking with God and responding to His call while doing the ordinary things of raising and providing for his family. This is written with a rigor and personal vulnerability that is compelling.

Stuart Wesley
Director Oasis People and Culture and former church planter and pastor

THE FUTURE IS
BIVOCATIONAL

Shaping Christian Leaders
For A Post-Christian World

ANDREW HAMILTON

Ark House Press
arkhousepress.com

© 2022 Andrew Hamilton

All rights reserved. Apart from any fair dealing for the purpose of study, research, criticism, or review, as permitted under the Copyright Act, no part may be reproduced by any process without written permission.

Scriptures taken from the Holy Bible, New International Version®, NIV®. Copyright © 1973, 1978, 1984, 2011 by Biblica, Inc.™ Used by permission of Zondervan. All rights reserved worldwide. www.zondervan.com The "NIV" and "New International Version" are trademarks registered in the United States Patent and Trademark Office by Biblica, Inc.™

Some names and identifying details have been changed to protect the privacy of individuals.

Cataloguing in Publication Data:
Title: The Future Is Bivocational
ISBN: 978-0-6453220-9-5 (pbk)
Subjects: REL012140   RELIGION / Christian Living / Calling & Vocation; REL074000   RELIGION / Christian Ministry / Pastoral Resources; REL109000 RELIGION / Christian Ministry / General.
Other Authors/Contributors: Hamilton, Andrew;

Design by initiateagency.com

CONTENTS

PREFACE 1
Formative Moments 1
Thank You 5

INTRODUCTION 7
This Is Not Second Prize 9
Could This Be You? 11
Towards A Bivocational Future – An Outline Of This Book 12
So What Is A Viable Church Anyway? 14

1: WHY THE FUTURE IS BIVOCATIONAL 15
This Party Is Over 16
The Perfect Storm – Christendom, Professionalism And Secularism 17
If Churches Were Hardware Stores 21
Are We Really In The 'Church Business'? 22
Is The Juice Worth The Squeeze? 23
Local Church Pastors – Missional or just Missing? 25
Imagine For a Moment 27
A Church With No Spectators 28
A Bridge Too Far? 30

2: TWO DEGREES AND A TRENCHING SHOVEL 35

Money, Money, Money! 36
Maybe I Will Start A Business… 38
Sweet Dreams And New Directions 40
When The Wheels Fell Off 42
Backed Into A 'Bivocational Corner' 43

3: MORE THAN A FAD – THEOLOGICAL CONSIDERATIONS IN BIVOCATIONAL MISSION AND MINISTRY 47

On Earth, As It Is In Heaven 48
Jesus Is? 50
This Thing We Call 'Church' 53
We Are All Priests 56
We Can Do This – We Have Done It Before 59

4: WORKING OR WORSHIPPING – CAN I DO BOTH? 63

Where Is God In Your Work? 66
Work As Cursed 67
Work As Income 68
Work As Service 70
Work As Worship 71
Bivocational 'Sentness' 73

5: TENTMAKING – IT'S NOT ABOUT THE TENTS 81

Many Kinds Of Tents 83
But Why Would You? Paul's Reasons For Tentmaking 87
Credibility 87
Positioning 88
Visibility 88
Freedom 89
Funding 89
Flexibility 90
Example 91
Generosity 91

It's Ok To Receive Support Too 92
Incarnation Looks Like This..95
Wherever You Go There You Are..96

6: WHO AM I AGAIN? VOCATION, CALLING & IDENTITY 100

What Do We Mean by 'Vocation'? 101
Primary And Secondary Callings 103
Fluidity In Calling..105
Impersonating Ourselves Or Becoming Ourselves?............................107
Beware Of Vocational Distortions 108
Bi, Co, Mono, Trans – Does it Matter?..111
A Process For Discovering Vocation..115

7: JESUS HAD A REAL JOB 120

Snapshots Of The Bivocational Life 121
10 Reasons Why You May Wish To Become Bivocational 126
And 10 Reasons You May Choose Not To Be Bivocational...............133

8: THE 'HOW' OF BECOMING BIVOCATIONAL 142

Pray 142
Conversations You Must Have..143
Where To Put Your Spade – Eight Options For Finding Work 145
What's Stopping You?..154

9: FIRST THINGS FIRST 156

Define Spiritual Leadership 157
How Do People Become Like Jesus Around Here? 159
Ministering From A Centred Life..163
Set An Appropriate Culture For Bivocational Church Life 166

10: THE NUTS AND BOLTS OF A SUSTAINABLE
BIVOCATIONAL MINISTRY 172

Teams...173
Build A (5Q) Team...173

How To Recruit A Healthy Team 176
Training Your Teams...177
Tasks 178
Do What Only You Can Do 178
The Two Essentials Of Leading A Church 179
Preaching – Sunday Comes Around Every Week 182
If You Have To Have Meetings 185
Managing Emergencies..187
Unavoidable Administrivia 187
If We Can't Do it? 188

11: NAVIGATING THE COMPLEXITIES OF BIVOCATIONAL LIFE 191

Tensions 192
Tension 1. Integrated Vs Separated? 192
Tension 2. Managing Expectations 194
Tension 3. Who Am I Today? 196
Tension 4. Practicing Contentment...197
Tension 5. Job/Career/Family – What Is This Thing Anyway?.............200
Tension 6. Is Sunday A Work Day? 201
Tension 7. Hours Vs Outcomes? 202
Tension 8. Resting Looks Different For Everyone...................................203
Tension 9. When You Hate Your Other Job..205

12: IF THE FUTURE IS BIVOCATIONAL... 209

Try It!..210
Teach It 212
Team Up 213
Persist..213
Who's Coming With Me?...214
Embrace The Opportunity...218

EPILOGUE 221

PREFACE

FORMATIVE MOMENTS

My mother once told me that shortly after I was born, the pastor of the little Baptist church we attended in Belfast, Northern Ireland visited and prayed for me to be a "fisher of men". Of course I have no memory of this, but as my life has taken shape I have occasionally wondered if his prayer may have been catalytic, or possibly even prophetic in shaping my hopes and dreams – of focusing my attention on those who are *not* part of the church and who approach faith with skepticism and hesitancy.

While I have been a local church pastor in various forms for over thirty years, I have never felt completely at ease in the pastoral role. I dearly love the people in my church community, however my heart is perpetually drawn toward those living in our neighbourhoods, who find the Christian faith incomprehensible, irrelevant or too bland to even consider. I often ponder what it would take for them to embrace a life centred on Jesus and his kingdom.

During my first twelve years of ministry I served as a youth pastor with the emphasis of our work largely on getting young people to come to church, commit their lives to Christ and follow him as disciples. This "attractional" model of church sought to manipulate the various elements of the Sunday gathering in such a way as to woo people into attendance. As it turned out we were able to do this quite well and the result was a large crowd of enthusiastic young people, many of whom chose the path of faith.

In 2001 when it was evident that my youth ministry days were drawing to a close, my friend and Pastoral Team Leader at the time, Garth Wootton initiated a process that saw him graciously step down from the senior role and take up an associate role alongside me as the new team leader. I discovered quickly that while young people were relatively easy to influence and impress, adults were not easily influenced and were very difficult to impress. Many non-church going adults were simply disinterested, or too busy with their everyday lives to consider investing time in church-based pursuits. I was perplexed as I tried to figure out how we could entice adults to come and be part of our church community. None of the clever ideas we attempted seemed to get traction.

I only spent two years in the team leader role, before leaving to plant a church, but during that time one of our pastoral team invited a prophet into our weekly staff meeting to speak to us and offer any prophetic insights he had for us. To be frank, I was fairly unconvinced that this person we had never met – and whom I perceived as quite odd – may have had something valuable to say to us, so I sat through the meeting relatively unengaged. He spoke to the other two pastors first and then my turn came. I wanted to be open and willing to listen for the voice of the Spirit, but I was skeptical. Then he shared the vision he felt God had given him for me.

"I see a beach with many people swimming in the water and having a good time but in their midst others are struggling and some are drowning. You are standing on the beach with others and you see those who are drowning. Those around you don't seem to see them – but *you do*. Does this vision mean anything to you?" he asked.

By the time he finished I had tears in my eyes and he had his answer. This man had captured my life's calling in one or two sentences. I saw the ones who were struggling and my heart was drawn to them. It had been this way for as long as I could remember. As my heart connected with his image, my mind turned to the shepherd who left the ninety-nine to go after the one. I began to make connections between various elements of my life that had previously puzzled me.

In 1990 I had entered Perth Bible College expecting to become an overseas missionary, but those plans came unstuck and I finished up the following year working as a youth pastor in my home church. I had really wanted to serve God as a missionary so I wasn't sure why things hadn't worked out as I hoped. Then during my years as a youth pastor I was sometimes criticised for putting too much focus on the "unchurched" youth and not enough on the children of church families. Coupled with this was an almost overwhelming desire to one day plant a church and have it function in such a way that it reached Australian people with language and practices that made sense to even the most unchurched person.

As I reflected on this prophetic vision I began to understand what had been happening. It dawned on me that my calling was *not* to be a pastor, but to be a *missionary*, just not overseas. I became aware of a deep calling to the western world – to be a missionary in my own backyard. I began to realise that mission work was *not* about enticing more people into church services, but rather it was helping Christian people embrace and live out their missionary identity in their communities and workplaces. Rather than trying to get more people back into church I was pondering how we could *send* church people back into the community as agents of God's grace and love.

When we began our church plant in 2003 I started a blog, which I titled *Backyard Missionaries*. I had hoped to share our experiences and learning with the people in the church we had been part of. I quickly realised no one was reading this blog, but in the process of writing I had begun to frame up my own identity in a way I hadn't been able to do previously. I changed the title from Backyard Missionaries to the singular *Backyard Missionary* (www.backyardmissionary.com) and for the last seventeen years this has been the forum in which I have shared my thinking and learning. I observed that over time other bloggers had begun to take the domain that was closest to their given names and I did consider buying www.andrewghamilton.com, but in the end those two words *Backyard Missionary* describe me so perfectly that I have stayed put.

While I am a newcomer to the task of writing books, I have been a surfer now for over forty-five years. I know there are some days when you paddle out and simply find yourself "in the zone". The weather is kind, the waves are friendly and you seem to be constantly in the perfect position as waves roll in. It's a wonderful and beautiful experience to flow with the ocean and to be in sync with such a powerful force of nature. Of course there are other days when the ocean is gnarly, the current is strong and you find yourself constantly out of position and unable to catch a wave.

The contents of this book have come about as I have found myself in the sweet spot of life; living as a bivocational missionary, leading a church, running a business and finding great joy and fulfillment in both. Discovering the bivocational path has been the key to recalibrating my life as a missionary and as a pastor. I hope the insights I share offer you inspiration and help in pursuing your own calling.

PREFACE

THANK YOU

An old African proverb says, 'It takes a village to raise a child.' I have discovered the same is true for a book. While my name is on the spine, the ideas I share have been wrestled around and tested with many other people, before making it onto the page. I am truly grateful to those who have chosen to engage with my thinking and offer both encouragement and critique.

Thank you to Coby O'Keefe, Phil Sparrow, Scott Vawser, Stuart Wesley, Garth Wootton, Andre van Oudtshoorn, Brian Harris, Rob Douglas, Alan Hirsch, John Olley and Jennifer Turner who read my early drafts and encouraged me to keep going.

Thanks to those who helped me with responses to my questionnaire. The insights were valuable in helping me understand how other bivocational pastors view their roles.

Thanks to Helen Bearn who was the first to give me direction and focus, and then Mindi Tognini who gently and capably guided me with editing and shaping the rough cut, second draft into something that is coherent and intelligible.

The gracious people of Quinns Baptist Church and Yanchep Community Church, the two communities I have been pastoring in most recently, have allowed me the forum in which to learn what it means to be a bivocational "missionary" pastor. Thank you for being churches open to non-conventional ways of ministry and for giving me the freedom to explore what it means to serve in these ways.

There are many others who have also been part of this process and I am grateful for your input and help.

Finally, my beautiful wife Danelle released me to pursue this project and believed in me enough to allow me to invest time and finance in making it happen – thank you. I realise you know all this stuff intuitively, and I have learnt more about mission from you than you may ever know.

INTRODUCTION

It was a warm autumn day as I strolled down to our local beach to check the surf. The weather was changing from the relentless summer heat to the milder days of autumn and my phone had stopped ringing with requests for sprinkler services. The irrigation season was coming to an end and I was looking forward to the slower pace of life that the cooler months would bring. I was keen to get back in the water and amongst the men who also surfed this beach as their local.

Upon arriving I saw the ocean looked like a fishpond and it wasn't worth the effort of running back home to hitch up the surfboard. Instead I swam out to the break just to cool off. I reached the reef where my friend Rik was sitting on his surfboard. Rik prided himself on having entered the water every day of the year so far – even when there were no waves.

'Oi – desperado!' I yelled to him. Rik laughed and then as we chatted another head popped up in the water and it caught me by surprise.

'Tom?' I said, partly speaking his name and partly wondering if it was actually him.

It had been over thirty years since we had seen each other, but I recognised the weathered contours of his face and that mop of blonde hair now inlaid with grey. He squinted back at me half recognising, but not able to make the connection.

'Scarborough High School,' I said. And it started to gel for him. 'Campus Life – Tuesday nights… Remember?'

In my late teen years I was involved in leading a Youth For Christ 'Campus Life Club' at the school I had previously attended as a student. Campus Life was an innovative outreach to local youth that gave them lots of fun in an accepting environment, but also helped them talk about serious issues and explore faith. From that time I remember a tall, lanky fourteen-year-old surfer with a thick mass of curly blonde hair whose name was Tom. He stood out because of his height and his hair. We ran that ministry for several years before all moving on, but occasionally I wondered, whatever happened to Tom, or Dave or Fiona? Where are they now?

I don't think he remembered like I did as he only attended a few times, but we laughed and made a connection. We mused over the Scarborough High School days, the teachers we had shared, and the era that was the mid-eighties. It was autumn 2012 when we reconnected. Over the ten years since we have seen each other regularly in the surf and shared some fun waves. I soon began working for Tom as his irrigation repairman. We have been to parties in his home and shared meals together. Tom became a regular client and he also became a friend.

Then in 2021 Tom got cancer. At fifty years old, in a second marriage, and with a two-year-old son, this was devastating news. While the prognosis is reasonably hopeful, it has still taken a heavy toll on this strong and capable man. Recently he asked me to install some irrigation and lay some turf at his Air BNB rental property. I went to meet him there on a 'bad day' after he had been released from an exhausting weekend in hospital. He was struggling to walk and needed to stop and catch his breath. I saw the raw pain in his eyes.

INTRODUCTION

Next minute I heard myself say: "Mate I'm gonna pray for you. Is that alright?" He knew I was a Christian but I had never broached anything spiritual with him before. I framed it more as a statement than a request because I saw his struggle and I wanted to offer him what I had. He gave me the green light and looked me in the eye as I put a hand on his shoulder and prayed for complete healing and a long fruitful life for him and his wife and his children. Tom's not a Christian, and I haven't made it any kind of personal goal to 'convert' him. He's a friend and I want the best for him, as I would for any other mate. The 'best' I had that day was a prayer for his wellbeing.

That story brings me a lot of joy. I find it wonderful that after all these years there is a connection again, but also because this story is borne from a purposeful bivocational approach to life. It is a way of life that allows me, as a tradesman, to enter a person's home and engage in my work, but also to come as a follower of Jesus listening to the Spirit and, at appropriate times, speaking, praying or acting in a way that reflects the kingdom of God into that space.

After fifteen years of running a small business, I have countless stories of this nature, where my work has given me genuine ongoing connections with people that my pastoral role wouldn't.

I never imagined this would be possible.

THIS IS NOT SECOND PRIZE

When I was a youthful 'twenty something' pastor and relatively new to paid ministry, I read a newspaper article about another pastor in the southwest of our state who was employed as the high school bus driver alongside leading his local church. I vividly recall a moment where I thought: "Wow – how sad! How did you draw the short straw and finish up at a church that couldn't afford a 'real pastor'?"

I felt pity for this pastor. I assumed that the only reason anyone would choose to work outside of the church was to pay the bills – to survive. It didn't enter my mind that the pastor may have loved his bus run; that it may have tuned him in to every family in the town; that he got to hear people's stories; and that some days it may even have been more enjoyable and life-giving than his official pastoral role. I had concluded that the right way to pastor was to do it 'full-time' and that other work was a distraction, especially something as mundane as driving a bus.

Thirty years on I have come to view church leadership very differently. Now I wonder, why don't more pastors drive buses, clean classrooms, mow lawns, or work in other trades and professions alongside their church role? Why is 'full-time' pastoring perceived as the preferred outcome for a person with a sense of calling to vocational ministry? And of those who find themselves wearing two different hats for employment, why are they sometimes taken less seriously than those pastors who are 'full-time'?

In 2009 my own life changed in many ways, one of which was to actively pursue the development of an irrigation business that, until that point, had been little more than a hobby. After six years of missional church planting, I was going to be working two days a week as the Pastoral Team Leader of a small local church in the northern suburbs of Perth. I needed to find the equivalent of another three days a week income to keep our heads above water. Danelle and I hoped that this fledgling owner-operator irrigation business was going to be the source of those funds. Our business started as simply a way to pay the bills; however, as time went on I began to appreciate some of what that other pastor may have felt as he drove his bus each day. I began to meet people in my own community, with whom I would not have crossed paths as a pastor.

In this new phase of life, my perception of work and ministry changed dramatically and it inspired me to reimagine what may be possible for those of us who serve in part-time church roles. Perhaps our goal ought *not* to be full-time employment in the church. Perhaps God is wanting to inspire pastors to work in trades, professions and business roles, to help reform our imagination of what it means to be the leaders of Christian communities in the years that lie ahead.

I hope that this book will offer a taste of what may be possible if we can straddle both spaces effectively to bring new energy and vision to both the church and the workplace. I am convinced that this is not a quirky alternative for pastors to consider in the years ahead, but instead will become the default ministry mode for those committed to healthy missional engagement with a post-Christian world.

COULD THIS BE YOU?

Student – Perhaps you are studying at a Bible College or seminary and contemplating a future in local church ministry but you don't see many opportunities opening up – at least none of the kind that would entice you. You're wondering what that means. I hope this book will give you a vision of what may be possible if you are willing to relinquish the goal of being a 'full-time' pastor.

Dissatisfied Pastor – Not all dissatisfaction is bad. Sometimes it is the Spirit's stirring to move in a new direction. Maybe you currently lead a church where you are a bad fit, but you have to make it work because that money pays your bills, and you literally cannot afford to leave. You may be a pastor who feels trapped in 'church world' and your contact with everyday life seems to have evaporated. You'd like to re-engage with your local community in a more significant way than simply joining the local footy team or book club, and you have a hunch that your skills in other areas – maybe a trade you once had, or a profession you were once in – would enable you to serve the community. This would also free you from being endlessly bound up in church activities. I hope this book will inspire you to courageously pursue a way of pastoring that allows you to be present in your community in a more substantial way.

Church Planter – Are you a church planter wondering: *How do I support myself as this new venture gets off the ground? What can I do that pays the bills, but doesn't draw attention away from my calling?* You realise you will need to support yourself for a time but, perhaps rather than seeing your non-church role as a 'vocational waiting room', you could intentionally see your workplace as a missional context, where you are able to live out the good news of the God's kingdom and practice the very things you will be teaching your church community.

Local Church Leader – Or perhaps you're a leader in a church where your pastor is bivocational and sometimes it doesn't feel like a 'real' church. He or she is not always available; in fact some days they just don't answer the phone. The church doesn't have all the programs and activities of the larger churches nearby, and you're wondering if you can still be a member of a community led by a 'part timer' – a part-timer who sometimes appears to be more invested in their other role than in leading your church. Is your pastor the real deal? I hope this book will give you a vision of what he or she may be able to accomplish, were they to explore a different way of doing mission and ministry.

TOWARDS A BIVOCATIONAL FUTURE – AN OUTLINE OF THIS BOOK

My intention is that this book will inspire people to consider both pastoral ministry and church planting as roles that can be undertaken alongside either regular employment, or the running of a business. It assumes that neither engineering nor pastoring is a higher calling, but that both are equally valid and important as a vocational choice, and that the future

INTRODUCTION

shape of pastoral ministry in the Western world will be *increasingly bivocational*. This may not be immediately apparent to you, but let me encourage you to sit with the possibility a little longer, to read further in this book, to imagine and then see what may come into focus.

In the chapters that follow we will consider a number of issues and challenges for the twenty-first century church that would point to the bivocational expression of church leadership being more suited to the missional context at this point in history.

The first section of the book will explore the 'why' of bivocational ministry as well as some of the paradigmatic concepts that frame it. The second section will dig deeper into what we mean by work, worship, and vocation, and will provide a broader understanding of these core concepts. The final section is intensely practical, offering ideas for effective ministry and drawing on the experiences of pastors who have either been bivocational or are currently serving in this way.

Some of the subjects we will explore include:

- Why should we consider bivocational mission and ministry as the preferred way of leading churches in the years ahead?
- How might a bivocational approach provide courageous, agile and competent missional leadership to the church in a post-Christendom world?
- What exactly do we mean by 'vocation', and what does it mean to be 'bivocational'?
- What is the biblical basis for being bivocational, and why have we generally preferred to take the 'fully funded' route?
- How is the development of bivocational leaders a key in forming inspirational, incarnational communities of hope in an increasingly professionalised, consumer-driven church landscape?

- How may we organise bivocational pastoral teams to lead the church more effectively than one person ever could?
- How do bivocational pastors navigate the complexities and challenges that go with this approach to church leadership?

At the end of each chapter will be a series of questions to enable further reflection. I suggest you use it as a kick-start for journaling, for giving shape to conversations with a coach or supervisor, or for a small group discussion with other pastors.

SO WHAT IS A VIABLE CHURCH ANYWAY?

In 2003 as I was on the cusp of planting a new church, I sat with our denominational leader to share some of my hopes and dreams. While he genuinely encouraged my ventures, he was also quick to advise me that a viable church had one hundred members and that I needed to grow my congregation to this point as soon as possible. I had never heard of a 'viable church' before so I pushed back on what seemed a rather arbitrary definition. Where had he located this his definition in scripture? He advised me that one hundred members *wasn't* biblical; it was simply the number of people needed to pay the salary of a full-time pastor.

I was both bemused and disturbed at his thinking. He might have been accurate with his estimation of the member to pastor ratio required to fund a single full-time equivalent pastoral role. However, I invite you to consider that a 'viable church' (if there is even such a thing) is far more concerned with the tangible expressions of the kingdom of God within the local community than with the ability to support one person in leadership. I believe the bivocational approach is the mode that will serve a truly missional church most effectively both now and into the future.

1

WHY THE FUTURE IS BIVOCATIONAL

In April 2021 my wife, Danelle and I set off for six months of long service leave, originally intended as a grand adventure across several continents, but reduced to another caravan trip around our own country due to the effects of COVID 19. One chilly evening in South Australia, I was casually surfing Gumtree, checking out what curious items might be for sale in remote country towns, when I came across an advertisement for an old weatherboard church building. It was in a small farming community nearby and the whole property was selling for just $65K.

This was the first time I had seen an actual 'church' for sale but, as we travelled through the eastern states of Australia, we observed many of these older church buildings now converted into private homes, Airbnb, art galleries, and cafes. I discovered a Facebook group called 'church buildings for sale in Australia', and I quickly realised there were many other groups like this all around the world. While people may not want to worship in these churches anymore, there is a still a strong demand for beautiful old buildings with stained glass windows, sandstone walls and rugged wooden beams.

Most of these properties are in outback (rural) towns where the church numbers have diminished and a regular gathering is no longer feasible but, I began to wonder, how long it would be until this is happening regularly in cities. The sale of these old buildings isn't just about changing demographics in rural towns. They tell a bigger story of how secularism is impacting the Western church.

THIS PARTY IS OVER

We have known for many years now that the period we called 'Christendom', a 1700-year era of privilege and status for the church, is coming to an end. Our prophets have been telling us for decades that we must re-think our approach to church if we are to survive in an increasingly secular culture, but the reality is only just beginning to sink in.

The 'party' is over. These older churches, being sold off and re-purposed are just an early indicator.

Christendom has passed and, while there may be some residual cultural memory in older peoples' minds, the next generation does not share their expectation of attending church or aligning as 'Christian' in any way.[1] Many Western countries have already been forced to contend with the impact of a world that no longer regards the church with the same esteem it once did. While the US church may appear to have negated the trend, recent statistics reveal that less than half of Americans attend church. The trend is for further decline.[2]

What does this have to do with bivocational mission and ministry?

I believe we must respond to this changing culture with some significant changes of our own, one of which is to re-think our inherited commitment to pastors being employed full-time as the norm. With a full-time, pastoral role comes certain expectations of how a church will operate and what a pastor will do – expectations that potentially limit the church's capacity to respond missionally to its context.

I don't believe the bivocational approach is a 'one size fits all' solution, nor is it the answer to the decline of the Western church. There simply is no *one* answer to the challenges we face, but this is a largely untested approach that could disrupt the current system in a healthy way and bear valuable fruit.

It often feels like those who have chosen the bivocational path have done so purely because the church couldn't afford a full-time worker and we have generally seen this as a temporary arrangement, or as a stepping stone to a full-time ministry position. My own experience also began this way but, as time went on, I began to discover the incredible value to church, community and my own leadership as I embraced this new direction.

THE PERFECT STORM – CHRISTENDOM, PROFESSIONALISM AND SECULARISM

Several years ago I went fishing with my friend Stuart and his two sons in waters that are normally calm and perfectly safe. On this day, however, the southerly wind was blowing hard and the ocean was choppy. We anchored around one hundred metres from the large wooden jetty and began casting for fish, not realising that the sand anchor was slipping, and the wind was shunting our boat closer and closer to the rugged timber piers. As soon as I realised what was happening, I tried to start the motor and move us away from danger, but my normally reliable Johnson outboard flooded and refused to fire. We were still drifting, so I turned to the auxiliary motor. By this time we were literally within metres of the jetty. In the panic, I didn't realise I had left it in gear, so it also failed to start. With both motors out of action, and the anchor refusing to hold, we were quite literally at the mercies of the ocean. It was a frightening moment, and I envisaged the boat being smashed to pieces and us swimming for shore. We sent ten-year-old Jordan under cover of the deck with three-year old Micah while Stuart and I tried to guide the large fibreglass vessel between the piers. Miraculously we made it through the jetty with virtually no damage to person or property, but it was a reminder of how quickly familiar and favourable conditions can morph and combine to create a perfect storm.

In a similar vein, the church has long been anchored in the calm, safe harbour of Christendom. In this time pastors have evolved to become trained and qualified professionals, whose job it is to ensure the organisation performs its core business efficiently and correctly. While different denominations might debate what that 'business' is, there is no question that a lot of it has revolved around the Sunday worship event. Up until the early eighties, there was minimal strategic thought given to how churches were organised beyond gathering on Sundays for worship and Wednesday evenings for Bible study and prayer. Christendom really only needed a pastor/teacher to keep the system ticking along.

While the Christendom anchor held, the role of the professional pastor was to give oversight and often 'in person' leadership to the core activities of the church. Pastors led the worship, preached the sermons, visited the people, and dealt with the personal needs of the flock.[3] We expected these men, who were usually solo pastors, to manage all of this because they had been trained for it.[4] Over the 1700 years of Christendom, we came to see this as the normal – perhaps even the correct way to lead churches.

In the late twentieth century our tried and true measures for running a church began to splutter and fail. People started disappearing from church, first in dribbles and then in droves. It started with the 'nominals', those who were present because it was culturally expected. Before long, though, it spread so that those who previously attended weekly only came fortnightly, or even less frequently. The mood was changing, and people now felt they had the freedom to skip Sundays or stop attending altogether. A serious storm was brewing and the Christendom anchor was beginning to slip.

People also stopped viewing the church as the first port of call when seeking spiritual insight, and they began exploring other spiritualties. Eventually we realised that the church was significantly out of touch with the culture, so we reasoned that one of the keys to regaining ground was ensuring what we did was 'relevant' to the people we were hoping would come (back). It was also the era of trying to work out what people's 'felt needs' were, and then meeting these with various programs.

In short, it was the beginning of our wrestle with consumerism as we sought to attract people back to the building. I'm sure this had already been happening in subtle ways, but the hard reality for anyone wanting to join the church prior to the '70s was that they needed to conform to *our* standards if they wanted in. Today we speak of 'belonging, believing and then behaving' in that order. You are welcome as you are. However, in that era you donned a collared shirt, stubbed out your cigarette by the car door, popped a breath freshener, and then spruced yourself up. Then you were welcome at the gathering. You behaved right (even if you had to pretend), secondly you believed our stuff and, finally, you belonged to our community. It wasn't very Jesus-like at all, but that's what happens in a Christendom-based world, where the religious institution called the shots.

As church numbers declined further, we were forced to further adjust our posture. This began by focusing much of our energy on attracting people to the Sunday gathering. We preached topical sermons on family issues, we spruced up the building, created visitors' car-parks, and so it went on. I don't know if we were ever aware that the anchor had lost its grip completely, and this 'perfect storm' of secularism, professionalised ministry, and consumer culture, were now shunting us at a rapid pace towards disaster.

In the early nineties something shifted in the DNA of the church as we tried everything we could to avoid disaster. Now, instead of being pastors and teachers, our leaders were told that they needed to be visionaries, marketers and strategists, with a five-year plan for the future of the church. We didn't just *learn* from the corporate world – we swallowed their methods in one desperate gulp.

One of the unavoidable consequences of 'marketing' the church, and appealing to felt needs, was the emergence of competition between churches. You simply can't adopt business methodologies and marketing strategies without hoping to beat the guy down the road. I know we nodded, winked and spoke of it being 'all for the kingdom', but the reality was that the vast majority of churches were seeking to carve out their market share to ensure the enterprise remained viable. In some church circles, people were even referred to as 'giving units', and budgets were forecast based on the projected income from those 'units'. While the pragmatists kept building their ecclesial empires, the purists were aware that there was something bizarrely abhorrent about what 'church' had become.

When the need for funds begins to drive your approach to ministry, and you are compelled to compete for your share of the market, utilising the latest corporate strategies and hacks, it is a sign that all is not well. While the adoption of business practices left a bad taste in many pastors' mouths, it was one of the stark realities of operating as a professionalised church in a post-Christendom era.

In his book, *BiVO*, Hugh Halter questions various assumptions we have brought to our understanding of church, particularly the importance of a full-time pastor to the legitimacy of a ministry, and the economic impact this has on a congregation. Halter calls for a return to the bivocational model that sustained missionaries and pastors in a previous era, as he believes this is our most effective way forward both biblically and practically.[5]

But can anyone even remember what that model of ministry looked like?

IF CHURCHES WERE HARDWARE STORES

Mike Tyson once said: 'everyone has a plan until they get punched in the face'. I guess he would know… Right now the church is getting punched in the face and the plan is looking shaky. Those who have hired competent marketing staff are continuing to expand their enterprise while eliminating the competition. However increasingly the church landscape is looking a bit like that of the hardware store. We all know that sooner or later Bunnings/Home Depot, is going to land in our community and beat us on the bottom line every time.

Our culture, and to some extent the church itself, has raised a generation of consumers so we shouldn't be surprised when our congregations behave in consumeristic ways. In a 'Life and Faith' podcast[6] focused on the 2020 USA election, and the identity of so-called 'evangelicals', it was suggested that consumerism had emerged as a *more* distinctive defining feature of these churches rather than the generally accepted 'anchors' of conversionism, biblicism, activism, and crucicentrism.[7] If we continue with the analogy of the slipping boat anchor, then at this point we are getting buffeted against the jetty and serious cracks are appearing.

However, this is some of what the future holds. The mega-mall 'Bunnings/Home Depot' franchise churches will continue to squeeze out their competitors, with guaranteed best prices, friendly staff, and a massive range of products. The medium-sized churches will do their best to compete with this and likely exhaust themselves in the process, while the 'corner hardware' type churches will either quickly fold, or find creative ways to survive. This is less about the church finding ways to effectively engage its community in mission and more about ensuring we 'outwit, outlast and outplay' the other churches in our local area. It's like 'Survivor' for church communities – a brutal, but inevitable outcome when church is driven by market forces. The best products and services are rewarded with growth while the less spectacular decline and eventually close their doors.

That said, unless incarnational, neighbourhood churches continue to exist as prophetic alternatives to a corporate, competitive mindset, then I suggest that in the next twenty to thirty years we will see Western Christianity become so conflated with consumerism that we will lose any right to speak of the 'good news of the Kingdom of God' when the 'good news' we are drowning in has more to do with our own comfort, affluence and aspirational lives than any priorities Jesus spoke about.

ARE WE REALLY IN THE 'CHURCH BUSINESS'?

In 2001, Scottish theologian, John Drane, sounded a sharp warning that the church was falling prey to the consumer instincts of the culture. In his book, *The McDonaldization of the Church,* Drane applied the framework developed by sociologist George Ritzer to the church and argued that increasingly priority was being given to these qualities:

- Efficiency
- Calculability
- Predictability
- Control[8]

Churches were becoming enterprises and, while these four factors may contribute to the success of a fast-food restaurant, they should never be regarded as the pillars of a healthy Christian community. Drane argued that, as we moved towards a post-Christendom church culture, increasingly formed by consumerism, we would actually leach the church of its radical beauty and potency by employing business and marketing methodologies to attract people into attendance, and then sate their desires in the most cost-efficient way.[9] Twenty one years later we can affirm that his concerns were warranted.

As the times change and the currents swirl around us, rather than allowing natural selection to take its course, there is an opportunity to respond with a sustainable strategy for leading healthy, prophetic, missional Christian communities that do not feel any need to compete or self-promote to sustain themselves. One key to this response is pastors being freed from the need to 'monetise' the church, in order to generate enough income to sustain their salary. In my own experience, removing the pressure to generate income releases a pastor to lead with a clearer mind into a complex and uncertain future.

IS THE JUICE WORTH THE SQUEEZE?

An added complexity is that, in this increasingly secular era, churches have become primarily recognised by governments as not-for-profit (NFP) organisations and consequently church life has become more complex and difficult administratively. Compliance regulations in the NFP sector, the demand for policies and procedures documentation, risk assessments, incident reports and other administrative data have created a black hole of bureaucracy for churches. To master this takes time and money – and lots of it. Our ongoing liason with the state means church budgets are being placed under strain.

Further, while pastors in some countries are currently able to earn a reasonable income thanks to the tax breaks that were given to the early Christendom church, it seems only a matter of time before these benefits are removed and the ground will shift yet again. Churches will be faced with either significant pay increases or staff cuts as many will be unable to provide the equivalent post-tax wage.

Into this milieu add an aging boomer generation who bankrolled much of the previous era of church life and we find ourselves with an emerging generation who (we have conditioned to) think in terms of 'user pays' rather than regular, cheerful, sacrificial giving.[10] It's not that this emerging cohort isn't capable of generosity, but simply that they often prefer to direct their giving to specific causes rather than contributing to the organisational budget in the form of staff salaries and operational costs.[11]

We are in an administrative squeeze that is flowing over into a financial squeeze, requiring us to think quickly and creatively about how we sustain ministry into the future. We will need to both tighten the belt financially, and re-think our to approach local church ministry.

The bivocational mode will likely be thrust upon some churches and pastors but, rather than moving into this space grudgingly, I would suggest that for those who are willing to learn, there is an adventure to be had as this unfolds.

If incarnational, neighbourhood churches committed to local mission are to have any kind of future, then one of the recalibrations needed is around the place of the 'pastor',[12] or whoever the primary leader/s of the church turns out to be. While seminaries may continue to train pastors for a future in full-time ministry, I sense fewer and fewer churches will be able to afford such a leader.

Is it possible we could develop churches that are not dependent on 'professionals', who are in turn reliant on meeting their KPIs for ongoing salary? Having pastoral leaders who are *not* bound to the church for their income will be a key to leading with integrity and engaging credibly in the world around us.

Secularism, professionalism and consumerism may have combined to create the perfect storm, but it seems we still aren't ready with any kind of perfect response.

I would suggest that now is the time to consider how we can help our pastors shift their thinking towards being genuinely and effectively bivocational. In doing so we will offer a way for our small to medium-sized churches (the vast majority) to thrive and continue to serve their local communities in their own unique ways.

That is a pragmatic and, to some degree, economic reason for us to pursue bivocational ministry more intentionally. In the remainder of this book I will speak to the multiple benefits that come from this approach to pastoring and share some stories of those who are implementing it effectively.

LOCAL CHURCH PASTORS – MISSIONAL OR JUST MISSING?

Unfortunately, the professional pastoral mould created at the end of Christendom is now so firmly set in the minds of both pastor and congregation that it is hard to imagine it changing easily. Anyone who has led a local church would know that there are constant demands from both people and programs to invest large portions of time *internally*. The organisation needs attention, the people need care, equipping and oversight, and the greatest kudos usually goes to the leader who does all this well. The Sunday event remains central, and it is usually the focal point for a pastor's effort during the week. Few churches heap praise on a pastor who is seen spending large chunks of time with those who are not part of the church; in fact, this can often bring cries of neglect from the 'flock'.

But let's be blunt – we don't do things the conventional way because it is more missionally effective, or even 'biblical'. We do them this way usually because it is convenient, self-serving and familiar. The message is clear – that the pastoral need is greatest *within*. Try telling that to the shepherd who left the ninety-nine to go after the one.

In a post-Christendom world, pastors can no longer spend the bulk of their time caring for the flock, while allowing mission to be formed by a 'Bo Peep' mentality – leave them alone and they'll come home. They won't. People *will* seek out spiritual help, but the local church is unlikely to be their first port of call. However, if pastors have the time to lead the way in engaging with the local community and can genuinely demonstrate missional living, then it may catalyse a new imagination and culture amongst the congregation.

While the concept of being 'missional' has spread to virtually every denomination and expression of church around the world, the actual practice has had less effective implementation. Authors Mike Frost and Alan Hirsch speak of mission as the 'central organising principle' and argue that churches should form around mission and let their ecclesiology flow from their missional context.[13] In the early 2000s they asked the question as to whether that change in a church's orientation would come from 'evolution or revolution'. While their solution was clearly 'revolution' (sharp drastic change), the practice, by and large, has been to try and move forward by evolution. As a result, many churches are still formed strongly by an attractional, Christendom mindset.[14] They have embraced the idea of being missional in principle, but have struggled to actually move people forward in genuine missionary activity. We are now at a point where we seriously risk losing ground if churches simply agree to be 'missional in principle' but little changes in their actual practice.

What *does* it mean to be 'missional'? The very word mission comes from the Latin *missio* which means to send, so the idea of 'hoping they come' is completely contrary to the actual concept of mission itself.

When I ponder the biblical portrayal of mission, my mind hovers over three short sections of scripture that provide a broad framing to help us understand what we mean by 'missional':

- 'As the Father sent me into the world so I send you into the world' – John 20:21
- 'The Word became flesh and moved into the neighbourhood' – John 1:14
- 'Your kingdom come Your will be done on Earth as it is in Heaven' – Matthew 6:10

Of course, there are many other passages of scripture that relate directly or indirectly to the mission of God, but it can be helpful and pivotal to have a concise reference point and way of understanding mission. Those three sections of scripture teach us:

- mission involves being sent into the world as the people of God';
- mission is incarnational – it is done in person, up close and through relationships rather than at a distance; and
- mission involves sharing in the announcing and demonstrating of God's rule over all of His creation with a view to salvation and new creation.

IMAGINE FOR A MOMENT

Imagine for a moment that your local church announced that, effective next week, all staff were going to be bivocational, working for the church half-time, while the other half of their week was going to be spent working a job within the community or running a small business. The purpose of the change was to place these people back in the marketplace, not as wild-eyed, proselytisers – but as courageous, warm-hearted missionaries.

This would necessitate other changes in how the church operated. Perhaps more part-time staff would be needed to pick up the tasks the pastors could no longer attend to, or perhaps it could be trialed that the church learns to 'live with less' by way of pastoral staff. For churches with multiple gatherings on weekends, and the expectation that staff are present at all of them, perhaps the requirement could shift to staff being present at just one gathering.

If the parameters for pastors were recalibrated then chances are the congregation would get the message that the mission of the church was *actually* going to be given priority over the comfort of her members. This would serve to encourage those already moving down this path, while prodding those who are sitting comfortably and enjoying the ride.

Can you see the value of choosing the bivocational route?

I am convinced that if we are to genuinely embrace the missional paradigm, then we will spend less time trying to get the community back into the church and far more time *sending* the church back into the community. This must begin with our pastors being willing to sacrifice the comfort of their offices, and coffees, with church members, and moving back purposefully into the community alongside their congregation to work and serve and discover what it looks like to be missionaries in their own backyards. If the 'Word became flesh and moved into the neighbourhood', then we too must consider how to be present in the communities we are part of.[15]

A CHURCH WITH NO SPECTATORS

Remember the board game Pictionary, where people played in pairs, with one person sketching and another trying to guess what they were drawing, while everyone else watched? Often church is a bit like this. However, it ought to be more like the 'all play' moments in Pictionary, where everyone is involved in drawing and guessing and no one is spectating.

One of the significant benefits that can come from a shift into the bivocational mode is that a sometimes-dormant church, with minimal congregational engagement, is challenged to step up and function as a cohesive unit. The body metaphor Paul uses in 1 Corinthians to describe the church community means simply 'attending' a church should never be an option. Everyone has a role to play, and a job to do, in order to keep the body healthy. Anyone can 'turn up'. It's another thing altogether to discover your own unique gifts, and then to serve alongside the others in your community.

However, before we critique church members for their apparent indolence, we may like to reflect on why they are not as involved as we may wish:

- Have they have bought into a consumer model of church and do not expect to be active. Where did they learn this?
- Perhaps some *are* active in ministry during the week in their workplaces and communities. Are we ok with this being their ministry?
- It may be that the pace of life is more demanding and there is less discretionary time to make available for ministry. How do we run our programs with increasingly limited resources? What programs do we cull?
- Or maybe it is a reflection of our own complicity in creating a pastor-dominated culture. Are we guilty of doing too much ourselves?

Many pastors do more than is required, or healthy, sometimes because they want jobs 'done properly' and that means doing it yourself. All too often we hear of pastors who are overloaded, burnt out, and unable to continue because the workload is too heavy. Frankly, if this is the case then we are doing something wrong. We are either doing too many different tasks and need to relinquish some, or we are taking too much of the load on ourselves, rather than helping other people find their way into leadership and service.

Later in this book, we will take some time to consider the various expectations that shape the behaviour of pastors, but what is critical is realising that often it's our own dysfunction that sees us doing more than we should. If the job of the pastor is 'equipping the saints for the work of ministry' then why are so many saints 'serving' as cheerleaders to pastors who are unwilling to release control to them?

This isn't just an issue for larger congregations, where people can intentionally hide in the crowd. It happens in churches of all sizes, as pastors take on too much, and people are enculturated into a context where their contribution is to give money and attend when they can. The rich vision Paul shares of a body is one where every part is connected, where there is shared workload, shared joy, and shared sacrifice. This is a very real and necessary priority when the church has bivocational staff.

A bivocational pastor should be employed to focus on his/her strengths, and others should be either employed or co-opted to work in the areas where the paid staff are not so strong. If we implement bivocational ministry effectively, then we can help the congregation use their God-given gifts, both inside the church and in the broader community.

A BRIDGE TOO FAR?

It was the early 2000s when I stumbled upon the 'missional conversation' a growing community of like-minded people who spoke boldly to the post-Christendom context of the Western world.[16] It called for the church to rethink its approach to virtually *everything* it did, with a focus on returning to some of the practices that were so valuable for the early church in its marginal status.

Some of the topics of conversation present in missional experiments and new church plants included:

- Encouraging the activation of apostles, prophets and evangelists alongside pastors and teachers to form the DNA of a missionary church.
- Planting churches incarnationally rather than seeking to attract people into attendance.
- Replacing stiff, hierarchical leadership structures with flatter, more relational forms that allowed for more involvement of members.
- Letting the missional context give shape to the form of the church rather than imposing a pre-scripted model on a community.

When implemented wisely, these are valuable practices that will help churches in their missional endeavours. However, I am yet to come across more than a handful of people who will suggest that we also embrace the early church practice of communities being led by either part-time or voluntary staff, who also work ordinary jobs.

Is that a 'bridge too far'? And if so, why?

It has been said that 'it is difficult to get a man to understand something when his salary depends upon his not understanding it'.[17] Perhaps this may explain part of our predicament. The system works for those who are paid by it, and who also have the most power to change it.[18] Why would you intentionally subvert an arrangement that is working to your advantage? Why would you risk your livelihood? The reality is that we all have bills to pay and families to support, so the chance of us destabilising the very boat in which we are sailing is slim.

However, what if that boat is taking on water and at risk of sinking as it gets battered against the jetty?

What if the bivocational route is an opportunity to respond strategically to the context, to learn and lead in new ways and propel your church community into mission more effectively?

Would you consider it?

We have a significant challenge in front of us right now – to reimagine the church for a post-Christendom world. We cannot look away and hope the problem disappears. It is here to stay and *we* must adapt.

So *why* will the future be increasingly bivocational?

- The 'perfect storm' of Christendom's decline, increased professionalism in ministry, and our alignment with a consumer culture, have combined to put churches in both an unhealthy and unsustainable position.
- The bivocational approach is more sustainable, agile and flexible, allowing pastors better missional engagement with the community.
- The bivocational mode offers a way for the local neighbourhood church to thrive and minister effectively, without having to compete with other congregations for 'market share'.
- The bivocational mode relies on the priesthood of all believers, with fewer tasks assumed by paid workers and more participation according to gifting.

FOR REFLECTION

- Where do you observe secularism growing and spreading in your own context?

- How is the church community you are part of currently responding to the challenges of our increasing secularism?
- How is your own missional engagement expressed day to day?
- How does the degree of professionalism/careerism in your church context impact you either for better or worse?
- What do you see as the obstacles to bivocational pastoring becoming a preferred mode of operation, rather than being considered second best?
- What has been your experience of either raising or maintaining finances while pastoring?
- If for some reason you needed to work bivocationally where would you try to earn your income?

Notes

1. In the 1996 Australian census 88% of the population considered themselves Christian. By 2016 it was 52% and dropping quickly, but the 'no religion' group had grown from 0.8% to 31% in the same time.
2. https://news.gallup.com/poll/341963/church-membership-falls-below-majority-first-time.aspx The report stated: "In 2020, 47% of Americans said they belonged to a church, synagogue or mosque, down from 50% in 2018 and 70% in 1999."
3. A person licensed, accredited or ordained to serve as a pastor in a full-time role.
4. There were very women pastors in this period.
5. Halter, Hugh, *BiVO: A Modern-Day Guide for Bi-Vocational Saints*. Missio Publishing. Kindle Edition.
6. Life and Faith Ep. 211, 13-minute mark
7. Source – https://www.nae.net/what-is-an-evangelical/ accessed 17.4.2021
8. Drane, John, *McDonaldisation of the Church*. Smyth & Helwys Publishing, Incorporated (July 10, 2012)
9. 'Slow Church' is posited as a response to the McDonaldisation phenomenon – Source https://canadianmennonite.org/articles/slow-church-movement-fights-mcdonaldization-church Accessed 17.4.2021
10. Boomers cited as responsible for 43% of church income in the US with Millenials 11% Source: https://www.cdfcapital.org/generational-giving/ Accessed 17.4.2021
11. https://www.christianstewardshipnetwork.com/blog/2021/2/3/the-future-of-the-church-amp-giving-a-millenials-perspective Accessed 27.3.2022
12. Pastor is in inverted commas because it assumes that this is the gift most suited to church leadership and does not consider the apostle, prophet, evangelist or teacher. It is the word most used in common parlance so I will use it for that reason.
13. Halter, Hugh, *Bivocational: A Modern-Day Guide for Bivocational Saints*. Missio Publishing. Kindle Edition. Loc 165 of 1524
14. Halter, Hugh, *Bivocational: A Modern-Day Guide for Bivocational Saints*. Missio Publishing. Kindle Edition. Loc 165 of 1524
15. Brisco, Brad, *Covocational Church Planting*. (SEND Network Alpharetta 2018) p.24
16. Brisco, Brad, *Covocational Church Planting*. (SEND Network Alpharetta 2018) p.24
17. https://jesuitschoolsnetwork.org/wp-content/uploads/2020/01/Consolation-and-Desolation_Revised.pdf Accessed 15.5.2021
18. The 'system' includes the larger framework of churches, denominations, theological education and ongoing pastoral development – everything that gives people employment and payment.

2

TWO DEGREES AND A TRENCHING SHOVEL

'So how on Earth did you end up working in irrigation?'

It's another hot, sunny Perth day and the person I am working for has wandered into their yard to see what I am doing. Inevitably we get chatting. They hear that I used to teach Physical Education, that I am a pastor, and that I also fix irrigation, which I readily admit is an odd combination.

Why this? Of all things…

It's a fair question. Who spends seven years completing two university degrees only to end up digging trenches and fixing garden sprinklers in the blazing Perth heat? More specifically, how exactly did I find my way into a physically demanding trade at the age of forty-three, while also leading a Baptist church?

In my twenties and thirties, I held various jobs alongside my pastoral roles, but they were each nothing more than a way of making up the difference in our family budget. Had the church offered me a full-time gig I probably would have taken it without much further thought, but not so anymore; not since I stumbled on the bivocational approach to mission and ministry as a *preferred* option rather than merely a survival mechanism.

MONEY, MONEY, MONEY!

In 2007 I learnt a way to invest in property and make fast money. It was completely legal. It was easy and it worked. Man... did it work!

In the boom days of our economy, banks were falling over themselves to give money away in the form of extravagant loans. Somehow – as part-time missionaries – we managed to convince them to loan us enough to buy land and build a house, complete with paint, carpets and everything else needed to finish the home off. Not only that, but we also borrowed enough money for the interest repayments while the house was being built, all while having a mortgage on our primary residence.

In hindsight, it was a ludicrous plan. If it had gone badly we would have been bankrupt. But, because the Perth housing market was rocketing out of control, the land value alone increased by two hundred thousand dollars in the nine months it took us to build the house.

When you've been on a pastor's income for nearly all your working life that is a gamechanger. We sold the house in ten days, were instantly debt-free and still had fifty thousand dollars left over.

I had barely managed to catch my breath when we bought another piece of land in the same street and were implementing the exact same plan. But it was the early days of the worldwide, economic slowdown. The demand for housing stabilized, and even showed signs of going backwards. Over the twelve months it took to build the second house we slowly realised we wouldn't make a cent. In fact, we'd probably be lucky if we broke even. It was disappointing, but we told ourselves that, overall, we were still in front and called it 'a learning experience'. To help save money, I decided to attempt some of the practical completion work myself.

Despite sincere concern from my friends about my historic lack of DIY competency, I figured I could install sprinklers, soak wells, lawns and gardens. Hopefully, I'd save a few thousand dollars. So I set about this work, albeit with little real idea of what I was doing. I knew soakwells were large plastic containers to catch excess stormwater, and some serious digging was required to install them. I knew so little about this that I asked a local tradesman if I was supposed to re-fill the plastic soakwells with sand once I installed them. He laughed until he had tears, and I had my answer. Of course you didn't fill them with sand … what was I thinking? I just didn't know that. Such was my pathetic absence of DIY knowledge.

I dug several large holes, ran pipe, inserted the soakwells and filled it all in again. It was hard on the body, but definitely not as difficult as I had feared. I also felt strangely satisfied at the end of that day. 'What was that about?' I wondered.

The following morning I visited our local sprinkler shop with a sketch of the area we wanted to landscape and irrigate. They drew up a scale plan for me to work from, complete with a list of every fitting I needed. This was looking easy – just a case of digging trenches, running pipes and making it happen – kinda like Lego for adults. I figured that if I kept to the plan I couldn't go wrong.

It actually was that simple. I made good progress with the job until around halfway through when I twinged my back. I wondered whether I should call it a day and get the 'pros' in to finish, so I called the irrigation shop to ask how much it would cost to hire a tradesman to install the remainder. They told me the labour cost would be almost equivalent to the cost of the parts. I did some quick maths and laughed at how much they were suggesting. It was a large amount of money.

'Suddenly' my back got better and I decided to push on. I finished the job in a little over a day and was glad I hadn't outsourced it. Again I felt unusually satisfied and content at the end of the day. It was an unfamiliar feeling, and one that had me curious. Had I actually enjoyed this physical labour? *Why* was I feeling so good after a DIY project? The idea just didn't compute, but it definitely had me intrigued. While we saved money, I hadn't counted on enjoying the experience at all. I couldn't deny a sense of accomplishment, and even pride, although I wondered if I was just experiencing a sense of relief that I was finished and hadn't embarrassed myself.

At the time, my paid employment consisted of leading a small, experimental missional community while working as a coach to youth pastors. I was also leading both our state and national boards for the Forge Mission Training Network. As I took time to reflect on this curious joy I found in physical labour, I realised that the challenge with all my roles was that I rarely, if ever, got to complete something. So the sheer act of finishing a task and seeing something working perfectly was surprisingly fulfilling.

MAYBE I WILL START A BUSINESS…

I had discovered what countless tradespeople already knew. There is immense pleasure in working with your hands and seeing a practical task through to completion. I sensed that I needed more of these experiences in my life. Spiritual formation is never complete. Missionary work is always ongoing and often slow. As a naturally task-oriented person, I needed something in my life that satisfied the raw desire for achievement and completion. Around that time my youth pastor coaching role ended and I needed to find some new work to fill the gap.

So the evening after I had finished the project I said to Danelle: "I'm thinking of starting an irrigation business. It could be fun!"

"Are you kidding? Fun?" she replied. "What do you actually know about irrigation?"

It was a fair question.

"Not much," I said. "But I figure that if I stick with simple backyard installations I could fudge my way through and 'fake it until I make it'. I will call it Brighton Reticulation and I'll just work locally." I was serious. [1]

Danelle just smiled, shook her head and said: "Whatever…"

I, however, immediately opened Photoshop to create a flyer to drop into local letterboxes. I also designed a business card to give to potential clients, and a website to prove I existed. It was all very rudimentary and basic, but it allowed me to begin establishing an instant business presence in the latter half of 2007.

Then it happened.

Within two days of dropping a flyer in a letterbox, a woman contacted me seeking a quote for her backyard irrigation. I drove nervously to her home and measured up. I drew up a scale plan and took it to the local sprinkler shop where a staff member sketched a plan of the pipework and a costing. I worked out a labour component, emailed my quote and she accepted. This was getting very real…

Now I had to make it happen. I needed work boots and tools. I already had a trenching shovel, and an old spade that would do the job, so I grabbed some cheap boots from Kmart, loaded up the irrigation parts I'd purchased and headed off to work.

I was both confident and nervous. In my head, I knew this job couldn't be that hard, but my experience was non-existent, so I probably had no clue about the task ahead of me. I was trusting that the plan provided by the irrigation shop was going to see me through, and that my soft, keyboard fingers wouldn't blister up too much as I dug trenches.

It took me a little over a morning to install the new irrigation system in her backyard. When I turned it on to run a test, it worked exactly as it was supposed to, and she was delighted with the outcome. I went home feeling proud that I had completed some genuine tradesman work, and made some dollars.

Over the next few months, the phone rang several times a week, with potential clients requesting quotes for installations or needing repairs on existing systems. On a couple of occasions I arrived to repair a faulty system and I was simply stumped. I didn't know enough to fix the problem, and I had to say so and walk away. I pushed through the embarrassment of looking and feeling stupid, and pressed on, determined to figure this thing out. Sometimes when I was struggling to solve an issue, I would call the irrigation shop and pick their brains or, as a last resort, I'd Google the issue for a possible solution.

I operated in this way for almost two years, completing five or six smallish jobs a week and earning enough to supplement what I had lost now my coaching role had ended. Eventually the pace quickened to the point where I wrote to our financial supporters and told them we no longer needed their support. The business was doing well enough to support us. In that time I was also becoming aware of its missional value as I got to know more people in our community. On occasions I found myself praying for people, inviting them to church, or just listening to their struggles. I had often pondered strategies for making effective community connections. Now I was doing just that, and getting paid at the same time!

SWEET DREAMS AND NEW DIRECTIONS

The following year turned out to be the convergence of both dreams and nightmares. In January we heard of a successful property developer delivering his investors a return of forty per cent within twelve months. We investigated further and he seemed the real deal, so we chatted about how much we could invest, and even risk losing if for some bizarre reason it all went belly up. We then borrowed a large sum of money and entered into an investment syndicate with twenty other people.

Late one evening during that period I was surfing eBay looking at buses that had been converted into motorhomes and dreaming about how much fun it would be to buy one, take the kids out of school for a year, and travel around Australia. It was a whim, but I've found whims are often the birthplace of wonderful adventures. The only thing stopping us was our commitment to Upstream, the missional community I had such great hopes for but that turned out to be a confusing struggle just about every step of the way. After some discussion with our depleted crew of people, we agreed to wind up at the end of the year. It was the end of a dream and very sad, but it opened the way to take an extended break. We worked out that the money we had invested would generate $100,000 over the year, so we could afford to not work and enjoy a significant holiday.

With the closure of Upstream we were also wondering what was next vocationally, when a nearby church expressed interest in having us lead them. I had already preached there on several occasions, and connected well with the youth pastor. We shared our vision for incarnational mission, and a detailed document explaining our unconventional approach to church, thinking this would deter any conventional church from being willing to take a gamble on us. It didn't. We were offered the job of team leader at Quinns Baptist Church for two days per week. We accepted the invitation hoping that the kind of missionary impetus we had been unable to sustain with Upstream would be generated within this new community.

We agreed to a five-month initial test period with the church, beginning in December 2008, after which we would head off on our 'big lap' of Australia (now reduced to six months in a campervan by my more realistic wife) before returning to carry on as pastors. This was approved by the leadership of the church. Unknowingly, we walked into a divided church, where we became the spark needed to catalyse an intense time of conflict which lasted until our exit in April 2009.

WHEN THE WHEELS FELL OFF

Shortly before leaving to start our trip around the country we began to hear of complications with our investment. The global financial crisis (GFC) was hitting hard, and our money was now under a cloud. The company director assured me it would all work out and that there were no issues to be concerned about.

However, over the next few months as the GFC began to detonate around us, further calls to the project manager met with his voicemail service. He did not return these phone calls. By July we discovered what our gut had been telling us: our project manager had done the unthinkable. He had 'borrowed' funds from our account to prop up his other failing projects, but had lost the lot. Halfway around Australia in tropical Townsville, we received the news that our investment had collapsed, along with all our funds. $250K had just evaporated… In the same week, the divided church met to vote on our appointment, and we lost the vote. We were now out of work and deeper in debt than ever before.

I don't often experience anxiety, but I have vivid memories of lying awake in our campervan with my heart racing, wondering how on Earth we were going to repay this money. My mind began to fracture in panic. Anxiety was sneaking under my guard to create fear and uncertainty in me.

Danelle and I debated cutting the trip short and heading home three months early to return to whatever work we could find in order to start clearing the debt. I am glad we didn't make that choice. It was the 'trip of a lifetime' but seared with anxiety. Lying in bed at night, unable to sleep, I would repeat to myself: *No one has died. No one is going to die. You have just lost some money. It will be ok.*

It didn't feel ok at all, but the self-talk helped. Putting my problems in perspective, by comparing them to others who were having a much tougher time was key to helping me get through without being overwhelmed or succumbing to depression. As I look back on that trip now, I only have fond memories from beginning to end. It was a good decision to keep travelling, rather than press the panic button and head for home.

With a month left in the trip, we received news that there had been more friction at the church. As a result, we were re-invited to take up the role. In spite of the difficulties we had experienced during our previous time there, we both sensed God directing us back, so we agreed, unsure of what we were actually returning to.

BACKED INTO A 'BIVOCATIONAL CORNER'

We arrived home in October 2009 to a two-day-a-week pastoring role with the only other potential source of income being my fledgling irrigation business. I immediately switched from hobby mode to overdrive. That summer I realised this was now our primary source of income, so I did all I could to establish Brighton Reticulation as a legitimate business. I had never 'pressed the accelerator' before leaving for the trip, so workflow had remained a trickle. But now, as I did everything I could to generate enough work to fill three days of the week, the business began to gain steam.

Had we come back to the hundred thousand dollar windfall we had envisaged, I doubt I would have invested as much energy in the business. Nor would I have the insights I possess today. Being forced to make it work added a new dimension to our lives, one that took some adjusting to, but it has been incredibly rich and life-giving. Now I was meeting people I would never have made contact with any other way. I was now starting to appreciate why Paul may have chosen to remain a tentmaker rather than devoting himself full-time to church work.

While I had been bivocational in one shape or form for all but three years of my 30 years in church leadership, much of what drove my work choices in those times was the simple need to earn enough money to pay the bills. There was little theological reflection going on, but rather a focus on finding work that was enjoyable and somewhat purposeful. That was all about to change as I discovered the many benefits that came from being a fully-funded workplace missionary and, as I began to ponder more intentionally, the place of bivocational mission and ministry.

FOR REFLECTION

Kathleen Cahalan writes: 'Vocation is inherently narrative. Its first language is story.'[2] I have become increasingly convinced of this as I have reflected on my own journey. Take some time now to reflect on your own vocational and professional story, paying attention to where you observe the voice of the Spirit.

- Draw a timeline of key vocational/professional events, transitions, re-directs. What do you observe in the shape of your story?
- Either outline on paper or (if you are with another person) tell your own story of investigating or moving into the bivocational sphere. Was it intentional or accidental?
- Describe how you feel about either being bivocational, or being full-time in church ministry. Have you always felt that way? If not, what has changed along the way?
- Where do you sense the hand of God at work in your journey towards bivocational ministry?

- If you are bivocational, discuss what you have learnt in the experience of becoming bivocational that you would consider valuable to share with others.
- If you aren't yet bivocational, what would it take for you to move purposely and joyfully into that mode of ministry?

Notes

[1] 'Brighton' was the name given to our local estate by the developers. The actual suburb was later named 'Butler'. My business www.brightonreticulation.com was started initially to service the one suburb. In Western Australia the word 'reticulation' is used interchangeably with 'irrigation'. For some reason this is not the case in any other place.

[2] Cahalan, Kathleen A., *Calling All Years Good*. Location 184, Wm. B. Eerdmans Publishing Co. Kindle Edition.

3

MORE THAN A FAD – THEOLOGICAL CONSIDERATIONS IN BIVOCATIONAL MISSION AND MINISTRY

It was the early eighties when the church growth movement first began to take root and challenge the church to consider how it could more effectively reach those in its local community. In the two or three decades that followed, we saw seeker churches, seeker services, emerging churches, alt worship, café churches, pub churches, and myriad other forms of 'church' developed to bridge the widening gap between church and culture. 'Relevance' became the buzzword, and the goal was simply to try and attract people back to church with quality music, topical preaching, creative kids programs and beautiful facilities.

While innovation and creativity are wonderful and essential, the shift I am advocating – a move towards bivocational mission and ministry – is not a new idea or some sort of cute novelty to grab our focus for a short time, until the next innovation comes along. It is a biblically-based, sustainable, and very practical approach to the various challenges we face as the church in an increasingly secular culture.

In choosing the bivocational path, we can engage the culture more effectively, fund the church and live more fully as the people of God. Pastors will be on the ground as missionaries and will participate in the same world as the congregation. As such they will lead them into that mission work with a much greater awareness of the issues they face. In this chapter we will consider four core theological ideas that frame a bivocational approach to mission and ministry.

ON EARTH, AS IT IS IN HEAVEN

At the very centre of Jesus teaching his disciples to pray are the words: 'Your kingdom come on earth as it is in heaven'. These are purposeful words because this is his hope and dream for the world – that God's rule and reign will undergird and influence everything we do – that our collective lives will be tangible expressions of that kingdom and that all we do in every sphere of our lives will be shaped by a vision of a world where the kingdom has come in fullness.

What does this have to do with bivocational mission and ministry? A biblically informed imagination of the kingdom in its fullness is vital to serving God both within the church and the local community.

In a sense, the kingdom is an 'alternate reality' that we are privy to and participate in, yet it is also the ultimate destination; God's dream for His creation. Theologian, NT Wright has framed the Christian story as similar to an unfinished Shakespearean play in five acts. Wright suggests that the first 4 acts are: 1 Creation; 2 Fall; 3 Israel; and 4 Jesus. The writing of the New Testament constitutes the first scene of Act 5.[1] The task of the church is then to 'live under the authority of the story', and improvise the final act as it leads up to, and anticipates, the intended conclusion, which is the new creation or the kingdom in its fullness. The implications are significant and call us to live life accordingly.

Perhaps the radical and counter-cultural rule of God is best grasped by placing its trajectory alongside what we would expect to be normal in our world. Jesus does this in his sermon on the mount (Matthew 5-7), often called his 'manifesto' for life. He speaks of living in such a way that love for God, and love for neighbor, causes us to behave in ways contrary to what is instinctive. If we live in accordance with his kingdom, then all the key areas of our lives are transformed. We think differently about how we use our time, where we spend our money, how we view our work, and our relationships. God's Spirit is given permission to override our natural impulses and, as a result, we choose to live differently.

Romans 12:1-2 captures it well, calling us to offer our whole being as a living sacrifice, to not conform to the world around us, but to be transformed by the renewing of our minds so that we can live in such a way that honours God and shows Him to the world. If we can take such an eschatological view of life and consistently live with the end in view, then that mindset will shape our actions here and now.

In my own community, a local businessman lost a significant amount of money because of an employee who failed at his duty. He was well within his rights to sack him and find someone else, but he knew of the man's home situation, of some struggles that were happening in his life, so rather than fire him and add to his troubles, he chose to sell one of his personal cars to cover the loss. This is not normal business practice, but at that moment a follower of Jesus, inspired by the Spirit, chose to behave in a way that embodied the kingdom of God, rather than simply the culture of the workplace. As we choose to live differently in our workplaces we point to another kingdom and another king.

JESUS IS?

Grasping the true identity of Jesus is vital, both for our formation as churches and for giving shape to our interactions in the world. How do we see Him living and operating in the gospels, and what implications does this have for how we live?

Theologians will sometimes speak of having a 'high' Christology, where our perception of Jesus is largely focused on His divinity, or having a 'low' Christology where the emphasis and focus are on His humanity. Of course, both are true, but where we choose to direct our focus will have a significant influence on how we live missionally in the world. The greater our affinity for Jesus as God, the further He is removed from us and the more He is 'other'. The more we focus on Jesus as the 'son of man', as human, the more accessible and approachable He becomes. The Jesus who came and lived among us to help us encounter God was undoubtedly human – a Palestinian man who lived with all the frailties and weaknesses of other men and women just like Him.

Eugene Peterson has translated John 1:14 as: 'The Word became flesh and moved into the neighbourhood'. In doing so, Peterson captured the beauty of the incarnation and the character of a God who was willing to come among us in the person of Christ. Jesus didn't just mix amongst us as a detached, aloof king. Instead, He lived in a small town, worked as a tradesman and formed associations with ordinary people.

God knew we needed a person with whom we could identify, who knows life as we do because He has lived it. In His time on Earth, Jesus did not cloister himself away in 'holy' places doing 'holy' things. He was a carpenter. His hands would have been tough from physical work, and He would have needed to develop effective interpersonal skills to navigate the challenges of being a small business owner.

When we imagine Jesus working as a carpenter, we may envisage someone constructing tables or cabinets, but we should also imagine a business owner who needed to interact with clients, chase late payments, and deal with those who weren't happy with the quality of His work. Jesus faced the challenges many of us face day to day as He plied his trade.

Issler writes of Jesus' workplace and the use of the word 'tekton' to describe His primary tasks:

> *Though 'carpenter' is the common rendering here, tektōn could equally mean 'mason' or 'smith'(as indeed some of the [Church] Fathers took it); or it could mean that Joseph and Jesus were builders so that both carpentry and masonry would have been among their skills. Based on his extensive word study, Campbell suggests "builder" as the better translation.*

Jesus was a tradesman who worked hard in His community. This was what He was known for (Mark 6:3). Even when we see Him lay down the tools to start His 'ministry', His activities were not confined to the temple or the synagogue. Rather, He spent time both there and in the wider world He was part of. He moved from town to town preaching the good news of the kingdom of God and making himself available to all those who were in need. This meant associating with the disreputable and the marginalised. Jesus was just as comfortable among the rougher end of society as He was with any of the elite; perhaps some of this was due to His background as a 'blue collar' worker.

While Jesus was purposeful in his ministry, His awareness of the marketplace was obvious in the subject matter of His parables, with the vast bulk of His teaching centring on workers and business owners of various kinds: builders Matthew 7:20-24; farmers Matthew 13:3-9; traders Matthew 13:45-46; management Matthew 24:45-51; to name a few. Jesus drew His insights from the world in which He lived and He demonstrated His clear knowledge of that setting. He didn't seek to present Himself as a super-rabbi, far removed from the ordinary environs, but rather as one of them – a man – but a man who had insight and power that exceeded the normal. Jesus was fully immersed in his world.

So when He prayed for His disciples in John 17:18, He asked *not* that they would be taken out of the world, but rather for their protection from the evil one. He then went on to pray: 'As you have sent me into the world, I have *sent them into the world*'. Jesus modelled the life He called His disciples to, and then He commissioned them to live that life after He was gone. To live a life focused on 'spiritual things' and to lock ourselves away from 'the world' would be to miss the central message of the incarnation, and Jesus' call to His disciples: to be present and attentive to the work of His Spirit in this world.

Over the years Christians have regularly created 'Christian' versions of clubs, associations, and activities that already exist in our community. Some of it has been done in the name of mission, while some has been a way of 'coming apart and being separate'.[2] For some Christians 'the world' is a foreign place and to be avoided in favour of bouncing from one Christian social group to another. This dualism serves to work against Jesus' calling and example to be present in the world, and to be salt and light in the 'un-churchy' parts of the world.

When we take a bivocational path, we choose to engage in the world more fully by being employed in a local workplace, or by running a business. Just as Jesus was fully 'in' the world, so we locate ourselves in our world by working a regular job and taking our place as ordinary members of society.

THIS THING WE CALL 'CHURCH'

A couple of years ago my aunt visited Perth from her home in Belfast. We started talking about church, and I asked her what challenges were facing the church in Northern Ireland.

"Hats," she replied.

"Hat's?" I responded, desperately trying to keep a straight face. This wasn't what I anticipated she might say. "Go on, tell me more," I spluttered, all the while thinking, *Hats? We are clearly operating in different worlds!*

As she spoke I quickly realised we were also operating with very different paradigms of church. She spoke of the tensions she had experienced in her church, and of the raging debates about whether women should be permitted in church with their heads uncovered.

We have all grown up with expectations around what constitutes a healthy church and, the longer we live with a particular idea, the harder it can be to embrace change. Hence the thought of a church where the pastor/s are purposefully bivocational can be a challenge to our thinking, on par with a church where ladies don't wear hats. It could be a recipe for major conflict. So it is vital to have at least a rudimentary grasp of ecclesiology if we are going to break from the long-held church norms and move into unfamiliar territory – exactly what *purposeful* bivocational ministry is.[3]

The Greek word 'ecclesia', which we have translated as 'church', is not specifically a religious word, but rather a word that is used to speak of any assembly or gathering. That said, 'ecclesiology' is the word we use when thinking about the people of God meeting together. In a similar vein to Christology, it is possible to have a 'high' ecclesiology involving ritual and liturgy of a very ordered and traditional kind, curated by an ordained and qualified priest. It is also possible to adhere to a 'low' ecclesiology, such as a church that meets in a home on a Tuesday evening with no paid staff, little structure and organisation. The first-century churches were definitely more of this ilk with the Greek word 'oikos' or 'household' being used interchangeably to describe their form.

In his book, *Bivocational*, Mark Edington writes of the massive paradigm shift early Christians would have experienced as the first church emerged. As people familiar with the systems of Judaism and priestly roles, this new egalitarian community of people, whose identity was no longer wrapped up in a central location, would have been incredibly unsettling. And now, instead of having a small number set aside to devote their lives to priestly duties, *everyone* was able to share in the formation of the church.

Edington comments on this phenomenon:

> *Significantly for our purposes, Paul makes no effort to identify anything like a priestly class, or to identify families who would exert dynastic control over the leadership roles in the new communities. This seems notable if only because such a model would have been both familiar, and very meaningful, to Paul, and we may at least imagine that his reasons for departing from it must have been meaningful as well.*[4]

The early churches began with a DNA of shared leadership and member participation but, over time as Christendom emerged, they reverted to a 'temple' type of understanding with dedicated people being appointed to lead and administer the now special and guarded sacraments. While the early churches recognised that some had given their lives to the gospel and needed community support, there were no paid staff as we have today.

At its core, a church is a community of people committed to one another and committed to loving both God and neighbour. Many have written of how this takes shape, but what is not negotiable is:

a) The church as a covenant community, rather than a haphazard or occasional gathering of friends.
b) The central purposes of worship, discipleship and mission. Some have called this 'the upward, inward and outward expressions of church'.

How all this takes place is largely negotiable, and that includes how the church is led. There is no singular script that must be adhered to. Churches that have not been led by bivocational pastors may initially baulk at a move in this direction. It may be perceived as a 'step backwards' for the church, or it may be seen as unfairly increasing demand on congregation members to attend to the tasks that the pastor would no longer be able to do.

Most of our understanding of church is derived from our personal experience over the years. We naturally assume that our experience is 'normal' and maybe even 'right'. But the reality is that we can fulfill the purposes of church in many different ecclesial forms. What is most important is aligning form with context, and knowing theologically *why* we do what we do. Hence a strong grasp of what constitutes a church would be essential for bivocational ministry to have ongoing traction and credibility in a community.

WE ARE ALL PRIESTS

If ever there was a doctrine that we have paid lip service to, it would be this one. While this is apparently a core belief of most churches (it's written in the statement of faith) the daily mode of operation reveals the true conviction – that there are *special* people who do *special* things. We feel they are more called by God than ordinary people. By subscribing to the idea that the important 'godly' work happens in church, and that other menial and unspiritual work happens outside of church in the common workplace, we end up devaluing the kingdom impact of ninety-nine per cent of the workforce. The vast majority of our lives are lived outside of the church service, so living with the knowledge of our priestly calling is vital if we are to operate well in this world as the people of God.

Art Lindsay agrees and states:

> *The priesthood of all believers has been the most neglected central teaching of the Reformation. It is one thing to say that we are a 'chosen race', a 'holy nation', a 'royal priesthood', and an 'ambassador of Christ'. Yet it is another thing altogether to have our identities shaped by these truths so that we act accordingly.*[5]

During the 16th Century Reformation, Martin Luther argued provocatively that the masses could engage in priestly work, and that the so-called secular world was every bit as valid a workspace as any church vocation. This was a massive challenge to the prevailing thinking of his time, which drew a significant distinction between clergy and laity.

Interestingly, as we read the New Testament, we see that some people definitely did receive a level of funding from the church community for their work.[6] Paul's argument that a worker is worthy of their hire speaks to the presence of these workers, and to them receiving adequate income for their work, but it's not evident if they are 'on staff' at the local church that meets in Phoebe's home, or if they were giving oversight to a region such as Rome. It is quite conceivable that there may have been someone appointed as an elder across the 'tribe' to give oversight, teaching and leadership to the house churches in that region.

There is no question that even with some people receiving support for their ministry, the church of the first century was a far cry from what we experience today. The whole idea of the paid pastor, particularly the 'professional' pastor isn't a concept we can easily ground in scripture. It doesn't necessarily mean it is wrong, as every culture and time in history have sought to understand and apply the scriptures in light of their own context, and right now there could be arguments made that the church is better for having competent, trained and accredited pastors. Conversely, it can be argued that professionalising various aspects of church ministry has served to render inoperative vast portions of the church.

This dualism – the belief that spirit is good and matter bad – is as old as the Bible itself, leading us to believe that, if we can focus our energies on the spiritual, then we will have begun to live on a higher plane. Of course, as we do this we rank other forms of work in relation to this, with the closer you get to working in a significant church role the more holy you are, and the closer to God you must be. We may appear to have moved on in our theological understanding but there are still plenty being encouraged to give up 'secular' work and enter 'the ministry' with the implication being that it is a step up.

Alister McGrath counters this beautifully by saying:

> *There is no distinction between spiritual and temporal, sacred and secular work. All human work, however*

lowly, is capable of glorifying God. Work is, quite simply, an act of praise – a potentially productive act of praise. Work glorifies God, it serves the common good, and it is something through which human creativity can express itself.[7]

In Ephesians 4, Paul speaks about a community of believers, all gifted differently, using their gifts for the mutual building up of the community. Alan Hirsch writes of the fivefold gifting we find in Ephesians as forming the essential DNA of the church – that the church comprises apostles, prophets, evangelists, pastors and teachers, and we need all of these to form a healthy functioning community.[8] These are not paid staff positions, but rather they are the responsibility and privilege of all who are part of the church. We will say more about this in chapter ten as we consider the formation of ministry teams.

As we move further and further away from the familiarity of Christendom and into this new post-Christian era, we will again see the need for the full complement of gifts to be present in the church. The Christendom imagination has been shaped to see the pastor or minister as one who cares, teaches, visits, and exercises all of the gifts on behalf of the rest of the church, with occasional help from the congregation. However, this emerging context will see us needing to also appoint apostles, prophets and evangelists to churches to equip the saints for the work of ministry. I will use the word 'pastor' throughout this book when referring to the paid worker, but I do so only for convenience and knowing that, as I do, I am giving way to a typology I believe is flawed.

It seems we are now entangled in a broken system that has come to rely on the work of a few to sustain the many. Busy lives and the growth of consumer Christianity has resulted in many people seeing church as an event to attend, or a box to tick, on the journey of faith, rather than a community in which to actively participate. In many cases, Christian service is viewed as helping the church community perform its internal operations, so it may extend to greeting, car park attending, or playing music in church, but few are grappling with how their faith is expressed beyond the gathering in the workplace. If we are to take the priesthood of all believers from the ideal to the actual, then it will involve equipping people for *all* of life and seeing what happens outside of the Sunday church experience as every bit as important as anything that happens within its walls.

WE CAN DO THIS – WE HAVE DONE IT BEFORE

To develop a church that embraces the bivocational approach to ministry will require putting our theology into practice deliberately and purposefully.

We believe in the kingdom of God, and living under the rule of Jesus, but often our conversation about this is ethereal and intangible. If, as pastors, we can work in our non-church jobs in such a way as to demonstrate the kingdom, then we will model for our congregation what this looks like. We will also be familiar with the challenges they encounter. Our conversations about living missionally will be informed and sympathetic, and we will be better able to equip them for their workplace mission.

We believe in the incarnation. We celebrate it every Christmas. We believe God became one of us in the form of Jesus of Nazareth, but the challenge is to grapple with the implications of incarnation for our own lives in this time. If we are Christ's representatives here on Earth how do we live all of life in such a way as to embody his presence?

We believe in the church as the people of God, the tangible expression of His kingdom here on Earth, but we have become so 'Sunday centric' in our thinking that the richness of the full expression is diminished at best, or even completely corrupted at worst. A fresh imagination of church will be less Sunday centric, and will enable us to move into a secular culture with courage and the ability to adapt our expressions as needed.

We also believe in the priesthood of all believers, yet we retain special people to do special things on behalf of others. In some cases, we even call them 'priests' and they are recognised as those who are 'qualified' to operate in this way. The message is loud and clear that ordinary garden-variety Christians are somehow less suited to tasks of ministry, either within the church or the broader community. We must dismantle this nonsense.

FOR REFLECTION

- What 'fads' or passing trends have you experienced during your time as a Christian?
- Does bivocational ministry and mission feel like a fad, or can you envision it as something more substantial? Why?
- How would you imagine the kingdom of God is lived and demonstrated in a work environment outside of church?
- Is your Christology on the 'high' or 'low' side? How does this shape your mission and ministry practice?
- How do you imagine Jesus working in your job? What would be the challenges for him?
- How would you describe the ecclesiology of your church, and how does that affect your mission?
- What are your stated convictions regarding the priesthood of all believers? How is this similar or different to those of your church?
- How are these convictions worked out practically?
- What would it look like for your church to really take hold of these four doctrines and implement them practically?

Notes

[1] https://ntwrightpage.com/2016/07/12/how-can-the-bible-be-authoritative
[2] 2 Corinthians 6:17 (misapplied)
[3] As distinct from bivocational ministry that is simply engaged in because the church lacks the funds for a full-time pastor.
[4] Edington, Mark D. W., *Bivocational*. (Kindle Locations 1417-1420). Church Publishing Inc. Kindle Edition.
[5] https://tifwe.org/resource/the-priesthood-of-all-believers/
[6] 1 Timothy 5:17
[7] https://www.firstthings.com/article/1999/06/calvin-and-the-christian-calling
[8] Hirsch, A., *The Forgotten Ways*. (Brazos, Grand Rapids 2006) pp170-177

4

WORKING OR WORSHIPPING – CAN I DO BOTH?

A few years ago I managed to land a job installing irrigation and turf in a house that had been built, quite literally, on the beachfront. It is still one of my favourite projects, and the story that accompanies it is another one of the reasons I love the bivocational life.

As the job began, so also began a connection with a woman called Jane who was overseeing the work for a friend. Jane owns a home in our street so she is a neighbour, but she lived 'downtown' and used her home as a weekender. The property we were working on was owned by one of her friends, and she was supervising the renovation work.

In the seven years since completing work on the beach house, I had undertaken several other jobs for Jane, attended a street party in her home and developed a warm, neighbourly relationship. Then one day she rang and asked if we could meet to talk about 'a personal matter'. I had no idea what to expect, but I sensed she was somehow tapping into my other role of pastor.

As we met in her loungeroom, she told me the story of her daughter tragically passing away as an infant.

But she then leaned toward me and whispered: 'She's over there'.

I looked across the room to where she was pointing. There was nothing there. I was confused.

'Her ashes are in that vase,' she said, clearly seeing the need to explain herself.

'Oh…' I replied. Where was this conversation going?

She shared memories of her daughter for close to thirty minutes, although I still had no idea what she was hoping for from me. As she unravelled her story, it turned out that her daughter had died at birth, but she had never 'let her go'. The cause of death was an infection passed on from Jane's body, so she struggled with a feeling of being complicit in her daughter's death. While she grappled with the false guilt arising from this, she had 'kept her' close by in a vase. However she felt it was time to farewell her and she wanted to know if I would do a ceremony of some sort that both remembered her and 'released' her.

As I realised that Jane wanted me to oversee this occasion I felt honoured, but also a little overwhelmed. I had never conducted anything of this kind before. What would I do? Previous experiences of this nature had taught me to simply say 'Yes' and figure out the details later, so while I had no inkling as to what the ceremony may look like, I affirmed that I would be privileged to share in that moment with Jane and her husband.

She had come to me as her sprinkler repair guy, who she also knew as a local pastor, and she was asking if I would do something very significant and sensitive for her. I had never done anything quite like this, but I tuned in to her desire for meaningful closure, and went away to prepare some reflections and a process for her to participate in with her husband.

On a windy Sunday afternoon a few weeks later, we walked down to our local beach with her daughter's treasured ashes, and she released them into the water. She 'let her go'. As she did, we spoke prayers of both gratitude and lament. It marked the end of a long and painful journey.

Jane came to know me firstly as an irrigation repairer rather than a pastor. I don't think she would have approached a Christian minister of any kind. She hadn't in twenty-one years, but for some reason she felt safe to broach this matter with me.

Jane and I still see each other around the street, and I still fix their sprinklers when they break. We are friends, but we have a connection that has gone beyond just my role as their tradesman.

When I observe Jesus, I see him very down to earth and engaged with the people who were unlikely to show their face at the synagogue. He spoke with them in a way that conveyed acceptance, love and kindness. 'Of course we can remember your daughter with you.' Why on earth would anyone say 'no' to helping a mother express her grief in the presence of the God who loves her?

This is my work, and also my privilege as a bivocational pastor, to be always on the lookout for where the Spirit of God may be moving. It is possible people could look at my work as mundane and tedious toil. If, however, you change the lens and view it as an opportunity to embody the life of Christ in the workplace, then that gives new meaning to the task.

When we follow Christ in this way, the Imago Dei (the worker created in the image of God) is participating in the Missio Dei (mission of God). As someone created in the image of God, I reflect his nature by creating beautiful gardens, and by helping people find their way spiritually. I loved landscaping the beach house, and I also valued the opportunity to help a woman grieve. At the end of both encounters I felt great joy. I would even go so far as to call it a moment of worship. If we are going to take the bivocational path then we need to be able to see beyond the simple tasks in the workplace and see the opportunity to honour God in whatever way we can.

WHERE IS GOD IN YOUR WORK?

What is *your* work?

It's a simple question, and often the first one we are asked at a party or social event. It can also be a defining question, as the reply we give allows the enquirer to form an opinion of us. We may rise or fall in another's estimation depending on how we respond.

It is assumed we all work and that our employment gives form and focus to our lives. In society our work is commonly seen as a reflection of numerous other factors:

- **Education** – generally trades are perceived as 'less educated' than professional workers.
- **Social status** – typically a doctor ranks higher than a plumber in many people's perception of social status.
- **Aspirations** – a person content with a lower paying job, with few prospects for advancement, may be seen as less ambitious than someone with a 'career'.

Our work inevitably confers on us status, and communicates a certain amount of social information. Whether this is accurate or not is another matter entirely, but we do know that perceptions are formed based on types of employment. While society views work through this lens, the Bible takes a very different perspective and, in doing so, allows us to see value, dignity and significance in all forms of employment.

WORKING OR WORSHIPPING – CAN I DO BOTH?

WORK AS CURSED

Sadly, in my experience at least, the idea that work is 'cursed' appears to be the most pervasive perspective on work. It is derived from Genesis 3:17-19 where God speaks to Adam:

> *Cursed is the ground because of you; through painful toil, you will eat food from it all the days of your life. It will produce thorns and thistles for you, and you will eat the plants of the field. By the sweat of your brow you will eat your food until you return to the ground, since from it you were taken; for dust you are and to dust you will return.*

Work is often hard. It can feel tedious and sometimes fruitless. While there is no doubt that our endeavours now encounter various frustrations, we should also observe that work was given to Adam and Eve *before* the fall took place. It was God's intention for them to care for the Creation, for these activities to be a means by which they bear his likeness and for their 'work' to fill their days with purpose and joy. In Genesis 2:15 we read of God blessing the man and woman by putting them in the garden to care for it. They are given the honour of being co-creators and partners with God in this.

Hugh Weschel challenges the notion of work as cursed:

> *Work is not a curse but a gift from God given to us before the Fall. By our work we employ useful skills to glorify God, love our neighbours and further God's Kingdom.*[1]

The fact that work was 'invented' by God before sin entered the world allows us to view it as an aspect of society to be redeemed, and to be brought in line with the Creator's original intentions rather than as a dimension that is permanently cursed and therefore to be lamented and endured.

Work can therefore be viewed as inherently good, even if it is performed with an element of difficulty. If you hope to be effective in the bivocational sphere, but you see work as 'cursed', then it's time for an urgent rethink.

WORK AS INCOME

Work as income is a level up from viewing work as cursed, but it is still a utilitarian and joyless perspective. The Bible affirms that work is to be remunerated appropriately (1 Timothy 5:18). However, when work is viewed purely as an exchange of labour for income, it is perceived at its most base. In the end the equation that results is work equals money, therefore, *more* work equals *more* money. It contributes to the idea that life is about acquisition and upward mobility, and that work is simply the hurdle to be overcome in pursuit of this life. Often accompanying this understanding is the fantasy of 'winning Lotto' as an escape route from the drudgery of work.

A friend of mine is employed as a police officer in a remote town, and it's a demanding job in every way. He tells me that the work is challenging and the administrative requirements are swamping him.

Knowing this, I asked him: "Do you enjoy your work?"

"No, I hate it," Jeff responded bluntly.

"So *why* do you do it?!" I am genuinely bewildered that a person with education and skills is stuck in this rut.

"The money's good, the holidays are good, and every second Friday the dollars just roll in," he replied.

"Every second Friday," he repeated quietly to himself. This is what he holds on for – the fortnightly paycheck. The job gives him little joy, but it pays well and he doesn't want to surrender the income. He's not completely stuck. He's there by choice.

In my own community, the emergence of 'Fly in Fly Out' (FIFO) mining work has lured many away from the city into remote towns, where they can work long hours and earn much greater amounts than if they were to be employed in city-based jobs. It can be a fast track to wealth and financial security, but it is often a pathway to marital tension and family dysfunction. When you work two weeks away, and come home for one, it's hard to have any kind of regular participation in community life. Some talk up the value of the lifestyle, but any time I have asked FIFO workers, "if you could make the same money in the city working nine to five, would you still go?" the answer is a very simple "no".

Scripture does not commend the idea of work purely as a way to generate wealth. Proverbs clearly says: 'Do not toil to earn wealth. Be discerning enough to desist.' (Proverbs 23:4 ESV) Or in the more direct language of the Contemporary English Bible: 'Give up trying so hard to get rich'.

Further in Proverbs 30:8-9, we read of a balanced approach to both work and income that recognises the temptations of being either too wealthy or too poor.

> *"Two things I ask of you, Lord;*
> *do not refuse me before I die:*
> *Keep falsehood and lies far from me;*
> *give me neither poverty nor riches,*
> *but give me only my daily bread.*
> *Otherwise, I may have too much and disown you*
> *and say, 'Who is the Lord?'*
> *Or I may become poor and steal,*
> *and so dishonour the name of my God.*

Work is certainly a source of income, but any time that work is seen purely as toil exchanged for money it is immediately leached of its greater value. To be clear, there is nothing wrong with wanting to earn money. In 2 Thessalonians 3:6-10, Paul writes of the importance of taking responsibility for your own expenses. He states that he did this while living among them as a model of how life is to be lived, before finishing with a challenge: 'The one who is unwilling to work shall not eat'.

There is a very practical, functional aspect to work. Those bills won't pay themselves and sometimes this may be the only motivator for a bivocational pastor getting out of bed in the morning, but that ought never to be our sole understanding of work.

WORK AS SERVICE

Work as service is not a uniquely biblical idea, as many people would see their various jobs as being the part they play in serving the broader community.

Recently Danelle and I have been planning some minor building work around our own home, which has necessitated having various tradespeople come to assess the work and give quotes. Each of these tradespeople is assisting me with work I could not accomplish on my own, and I am grateful for the combination of skills that will transform our home into a more pleasant place to live. While I may pay them, they are still serving me by completing the tasks required.

This is a loftier view of work than seeing it as simply an exchange of resources, and one that involves an element of seeing another person and meeting their needs. Hopefully, this approach will already be in your sights, whether you are a teacher, a nurse, or a plumber – your job is to *serve* to the best of your capacity.

Work as service is possibly the highest view of work in the community around us; however, the Bible calls us to elevate our expectations even further.

WORK AS WORSHIP

When we begin to think of work as worship we come to the heart of the biblical understanding, and we position ourselves to find real joy and meaning in our non-church roles. It may be generally regarded as intrinsically more fulfilling to teach eager students in a university than to move barrows of dirt as a labourer, but both have the potential to be acts of worship if we can manage our perceptions and sense of identity.

Originally our work was intended to be performed in conjunction with the Creator, as we tended to and cared for the world He created. It was supposed to be a point of connection with Him. We see Adam and Eve as 'partners' with God in the garden.

The various calls to work in scripture are often in the context of honouring God with our labour. Broadly speaking we are to follow the instructions in Romans 12:1-2 – to present ourselves to God as living sacrifices, to not conform to the standards of the world, but to be transformed by the renewing of our minds so that everything we do, including work, is viewed differently.

Colossians 3:23 puts it most simply: 'Whatever you do work at it with all your heart, as if working for the Lord, not for human masters'. Similarly, 1 Corinthians 10:31 states: 'So whether you eat or drink or whatever you do, do it all for the glory of God'.

Interestingly the early Hebrews had one word that was used for *both* work and worship. Austin Burkhart explains that the Hebrew word *avodah* is used to refer to tasks such as farming or manual labour, but is also used to describe our worship of God. The use of this word to describe both activities suggests that they may be viewed in the same way by God. Burkhart lists several examples:[2]

> *Six days you shall work (avodah).* – Exodus 34:21

> *Then man goes out to his work (avodah), to his labour until evening.* – Psalm 104:23

> *This is what the LORD says: Let my people go, so that they may worship (avodah) me.* – Exodus 8:1

> *But as for me and my household, we will serve (avodah) the Lord.* – Joshua 24:15

Clearly, the original intent of the Creator was for our work and worship to be one and the same activity – for our service to the world to *equally* be service to God, and thus an act of worship. Theologian Miroslav Volf states that: 'the Spirit of God calls and gifts people to work in active anticipation of the eschatological transformation of the world'.[3] He is advocating for us to work in such a way that we point to the new creation that is not yet fully here, but will be in the age to come. It is a grand and inspiring view of work.

Perhaps the question for us is simply: *what does that look like?* For many Christians dualistic thinking has led them to see their 'work world' and their 'church world' as separate entities. At church they do 'spiritual things' and at work, they do 'employment-related things'. While they may adhere to the theory of all of life being an act of worship, the actual practice is sometimes difficult to implement. What does it look like to 'worship' God through a performance management process with an under-performing staff member? How is our worship expressed when we find ourselves in apparently pointless meetings with no escape? Or what would worship look like for a coal miner on a four week on/one week off roster working twelve hours days underground, in stifling conditions.

The point here is not to answer all of those questions, but rather to believe that it is *possible* to answer them. We can worship and honour God in all spheres of employment if we can discern what that means and what is required of us. To take this view into a bivocational situation is to believe that neither one of our paid roles is in any way more God honouring than the other. To be more specific, I do not honour God more when I teach the Bible faithfully than when I lay turf carefully and beautifully. Both can be acts of worship, but both can also be self-centred and self-gratifying.

Returning to my client Jane, I was worshipping God when I created a beautiful garden for her just as much as when I helped her mourn the loss of her daughter. On both occasions I sensed the nearness of God and his participation in my work. I believe this is what He hopes for all of us who operate bivocationally.

BIVOCATIONAL 'SENTNESS'

If you consider yourself to be a follower of Jesus, on mission wherever you go and expressing 'work as worship', then you will *never* see your work as 'just a job that needs doing'. We enter that workplace, not just as a believer but also as a missionary because this is what it means to be sent. Wherever we find ourselves working, we are there as the people of God; salt to add flavor, and light to show a path to those who may be in darkness. Our job is not to persuade people to come to church, or to get them close to a pastor so he/she can 'work their magic'. It's simply to recognise our own 'sentness', to understand *who* we are sent to and then how we can live and speak the good news of Jesus to them.

One of the key questions I feel we need to take with us into our workplace is: *if Jesus was doing your job, then what would he do?* What traits would distinguish him as an employee? We are possibly going to be the only experience of God some of our colleagues ever have. So rather than just waiting for an opportunity to 'witness' and then stumbling through a pre-heated gospel spiel, we are called to live amongst, to love and serve the people around us, and to demonstrate the life of Jesus in our practice. This is both worship and mission in the workplace – simply being the presence of Jesus and articulating our hope when called upon.

This isn't always easy or straightforward.

On one occasion I received an aggressive and manipulative email from a client I had worked for two months previously. It accused us of *not* completing the contracted work and of leaving his irrigation system *worse* than when we arrived. This was despite a prior email from him thanking us for doing a 'great job'. Now, he delivered an ultimatum: ensure his system was working as it should or he would leave a negative Google review.

My first instinct was sheer rage. His tone was pushing all of my hot buttons and I really wanted to email back and offer some not so loving correction. I have learnt that this is not always the best response… and probably doesn't represent Jesus very well either.

I paused, slept on it, and then wrote a firm, but conciliatory email, offering to fix any work no longer functioning properly, but explaining that we couldn't be responsible for new problems that weren't present initially. His return email raised the level of threat and was even more demeaning, rude and aggressive. He demanded we return at no cost and fix the issues he identified, but he 'knew we wouldn't' so he would be forced to contract someone else, video the work and then send us the bill. He would then take the issue to government authorities and seek some form of sanction for us.

Once again, my immediate reaction was raw anger. It was the tone, the content, the lies, the injustice, the assumptions, the… everything! It felt like someone was shoving their finger into my chest and picking a fight.

In all situations of this ilk, stepping back allows me a chance to breathe and to remember who I am. My 'higher self' (the part of me that follows Jesus) wrestles with my 'lower self' (the part of me that thinks revenge and instant gratification is a good idea). I know this, so as I step back, the question I seek to use in framing my reply is simply: *what would a Christlike response be? How do I honour (worship) God in this situation?* When these emails arrived, I was in the process of training my eighteen-year-old son, Sam, to run the business so that he could stand in for six months while I went on long service leave. It was a timely, real-life case study in conflict management. I gave him the emails to read and asked him to consider how we should respond. I heard him chuckle as he read them. "Is this guy for real dad?" he asked. Then we began to discuss how Jesus might deal with this.

We debated whether He would push back on bullies, as He sometimes did with the Pharisees, or whether He would overwhelm them with love and kindness. We agreed that if we were to demonstrate the kingdom of God to this man, then it would be through some 'extreme loving'. I sent a brief email to the client letting him know we would fix all issues at our expense, and we agreed on a time. A couple of days later we went to his home and, on the way, we prayed for grace and kindness to prevail. As we arrived, we smiled, shook his hand and greeted him warmly. From there we resolved all of the issues he described, as well as some others we managed to find. None of the issues were our fault and after showing him the actual causes of the problems he quickly realised he was wrong. Sam and I chose to be effusively kind, generous and helpful in the hope that he may begin to wonder why we had chosen this form of response. We agreed this was how Jesus would respond to him. And he *was* genuinely overwhelmed and bemused at our approach. After just ten minutes of enthusiastically sorting out his issues I sent Sam to the car to fetch a part we needed.

While Sam was gone the client began to offer an apology: 'Hey I'm sorry if I was a bit obnoxious in my emails. I've just had a really hard week.'

In this moment my tradesman self took a back seat role. Instead, I allowed my pastoral self to engage. "Oh yeah?" I asked gently. "What's a hard week look like?" I was interested to hear what had given rise to the rage I had experienced in his emails.

He went on to speak of some serious family issues that revolved around his recent separation from his wife. He was distraught and broken, and we had been unlucky enough to be on the receiving end of his anger. This man lived in the same suburb as our church. He didn't know Jesus, and he was someone to whom we could communicate the love of Christ. If that meant taking a few on the chin while we get close, then so be it.

As we left he grabbed my arm: "Ok, I need to say this. You were right. I was wrong. Thank you. I will be writing you guys an amazing google review".

It was a confession of sorts, a recognition of his own error and a decision to do what he could to make amends. His subsequent review was effusive in praise and acknowledged that the system was faulty because *he* had broken it himself. It was yet another reminder that we do not overcome evil with evil, but rather with goodness and love. In that time our work was also our worship as we practiced being 'sent' into the community as missionaries.

From time to time I have young men come and work for me. Whether or not they are a Christian, my instruction to them is to:

    a)   go about your work as you imagine Jesus would do it; and

b) imagine your client *as* Jesus and then serve them with that in mind.

This is the nub of mission in the workplace – to embody the one we claim to follow. When the word became flesh and moved into the neighbourhood, He lived a very ordinary life for the first thirty or so years. Ordinary enough that when people who had known him his whole life saw Him speaking with authority in the synagogue, they were stunned. They asked: "Isn't this Joseph's son?" Clearly He wasn't the Jesus they thought they had come to know.

As pastors in workplace mission and ministry, we simply have to grasp that our primary job is not to convert our workmates. To many, this is stating the obvious but, for some people, this is still their mentality when they approach any form of mission. In essence: *'I haven't done anything worthwhile until I have shared the gospel verbally and hopefully led someone to faith in Christ'.*

Mission is whatever we do or say to communicate the love of God to his world. Evangelism – sharing the good news of Jesus salvation verbally – is a subset of this and a vital part of the mission process, but there is much you can do to be 'missional' without needing to leave a 'Two Ways to Live' tract under your co-worker's keyboard, or seeking to swing the morning tea conversation from football to faith at every opportunity.

Let it go. Please let it go. Awkward, clumsy sales spiels do more harm than good.

While our greatest desire is to lead people to a place of surrender to Jesus and to follow Him with all their heart, most employers don't take kindly to workplace proselytising, and nor should they. We aren't paid to evangelise. We are paid to *'avodah'* and when we do, people will inevitably encounter the Jesus we claim to follow.

In the workplace, mission looks like this:

- working hard and doing a good job – this *is* worship and is the primary reason you are there;
- looking for where God may already be at work in people's lives;
- functioning with kindness, integrity and generosity in all we do;
- refusing to be part of dishonesty or workplace bullying;
- being the person who brings encouragement, joy and hope into the room;
- searching out for those who may be getting a rough deal, and helping them find justice;
- seeing opportunities to love, serve and bless workmates; and
- when invited, being able to give a reason for the hope we have.

FOR REFLECTION

- Reflect on which paradigm of work you most immediately identify with and why.
- How may grasping the concept of 'avodah' impact practically on how you work?
- Reflect on how you currently 'practice your faith' in your work context. What does that look like?
- What challenges do you encounter as you seek to be true to your faith in the work environment?
- If work *is* worship, then how does God currently see your act of worship?
- What does mission look like for you at work? What are some examples of how you have expressed your love for God in your workplace?

- How have you been equipped for this mission work by your church?
- How would you seek to equip those in your church for living missionally in their work environments?

Notes

1. https://tifwe.org/is-work-a-curse-the-cultural-mandate-1/
2. https://tifwe.org/avodah-a-life-of-work-worship-and-service/ Austin Burkhart
3. Volf, M., *Work in The Spirit*. (Wipf and Stock, Eugene, 2001) p.123

5

TENTMAKING – IT'S NOT ABOUT THE TENTS

So the big name in all of the discussions on pastors and missionaries having other forms of employment is, of course, Paul. It seems Peter and James left their boats and their fishing to follow Jesus, although clearly there was the capacity to return to them as they did after the crucifixion. We get the impression that Luke travelled with Paul and friends but remained primarily a doctor, while Jesus himself put down the tools to begin his ministry and relied on the support of others.[1] There are few places in scripture where we see how people's work, combined with their ministry, enable greater effectiveness in both areas. Paul is one of those people where we can make some observations.

We hang a lot on Paul, so much so that the only 'trade' that ever aligns with bivocational work is that of the tentmaker. Ironically, Paul was in no doubt that his primary sense of vocation was derived from the gospel – that he was 'the apostle to the Gentiles' and that all he did in this world was in the service of God towards that end. Paul is passionate and intense in his writings about what it means to know and follow Jesus, but he writes nothing of any similar significance about the trade that had been the staple of his life. It seems his tentmaking served, and aided, his true vocation and enabled him to be and do the things God had called him to.

When we use the term 'tentmaker' today, we typically mean pastors or missionaries who provides some or all of their funding by working in a non-church based job. This may be an intentional choice, as Paul's was, or it may be a simple necessity because the church is unable to fully fund the pastor's time. For this book I surveyed 25 bivocational pastors, and the clear conclusion was that all initially took the tentmaker path by necessity. Along the way, however, some discovered the joy and value of the bivocational path, and have now made it their first choice for mission and ministry.

In 1 Corinthians 9:12-18, Paul writes that his reason for choosing this path is so that he might not be a burden to the Corinthian church, or a hindrance to their faith decisions:

> *On the contrary, we put up with anything rather than hinder the gospel of Christ.*

In the first part of the chapter, Paul acknowledges his 'right' to receive income from them, but then states that he has voluntarily chosen to deny himself this entitlement. There is no sense in Paul's writings that this is to be a pattern adopted by everyone but, if someone as gifted as Paul chose to exercise his ministry in this way, then it makes sense that we pay attention and learn what we can from his reasons and his methods.

MANY KINDS OF TENTS

We need to allow for some fluidity around this concept of 'tentmaking', as the idea has been expressed in numerous ways throughout history. Right from the very beginning of the church, the bivocational experience has been normative. Early Church Father Tertullian (160 CE – 220 CE) was a serious advocate for those serving in churches to be bivocational. He is quoted as saying:

> *Let the young persons of the Church endeavour to minister diligently with all appropriate seriousness, so that you will always have sufficient funds to support both yourselves and those that are needy, and not burden the Church of God. For we ourselves, besides our attention to the word of the Gospel, do not neglect our inferior employments. For some of us are fisherman, tentmakers, and farmers, so that we may never be idle.*[2]

If you read that quote carefully you would have seen Tertullian refer to *our inferior employments*, perhaps a sign that the tide was already turning and that service to God was seen as superior to that of other work.

This pattern of ministering bivocationally changed drastically in 313 CE with Constantine's conversion. The subsequent Edict of Milan freed Christians from oppression and persecution, and virtually overnight turned them into a legitimate, fully-funded religion of the empire. Paid roles were established for both bishops and presbyters, and Christians were given buildings in which to meet and establish their churches. While they were no longer persecuted, the alignment with the Roman Empire brought a different set of challenges. Missiologist Darrell Guder writes:

> *No longer based on gift and function, ordination was state-sanctioned and institutionalised office was gained through rank and study. Clerical embodiment of the means of grace and office defined the church. The governing principle became, 'No clergy, no church'.*[3]

While this became the default mode of church from that time on, there were still those who chose the bivocational pathway. William Carey is an oft-cited example of a man with a clear missionary vocation who chose to work in secular jobs as a means of self-funding. According to Patrick Lai:

> *William Carey, the father of the modern missionary movement, was a tentmaker. When the British East India Company would not allow Carey to work as a missionary, he took employment in a location outside of their control. When he or his co-workers' funds ran low, he found employment to supplement their needs. During his career in India, Carey worked as a translator, cobbler, factory manager, educator and journalist. He said, 'My business is to witness for Christ, I make shoes just to pay my expenses.'*[4]

Even today, for many missionaries, the only way to gain access to otherwise 'closed' countries is by finding a job to sustain themselves while they build relationships and engage in careful evangelism. The tentmaker model is the primary way of engaging in mission with countries where proselytising is against the law.

Closer to my own home, William Kennedy, a pioneer of rural Western Australian Baptist churches in the 1890s, was also largely self-funded after arriving in the small rural town of Katanning to discover that his new church family could not actually afford to pay him a wage that would sustain him. He was paid a pittance and given an old bicycle as his primary mode of transport. He made up the deficit with other work he sourced around the town, often farm work that enabled him to serve the local people and become part of their lives.

In the late nineties, Chris Robinson began the work of Quinns Baptist Church, the community Danelle and I are currently pastors in. Chris worked various jobs, including as a real estate salesperson and a bus driver, to provide for his family while also pioneering the church and, later, giving oversight to beginnings of Quinns Baptist College. As with so many pioneers, there was significant personal sacrifice involved in such a venture. Long days of bus driving became even longer as going home meant meeting with church people.

In yet a different situation, Andy Pitt of Down South Gospel Church in rural Busselton moved from a full-time pastoral role to working four days in the church and one in the local aluminium mine. Financial pressures within the church necessitated the move, but Andy has found it to be a valuable source of income as well as enabling him to connect in more significant ways with the men in his community. The tentmaking component of income is only one fifth of his working week, but Andy would say that the benefits to his ministry are significant, suggesting that when a person enters a tentmaking space with a focused missionary heart the work is somewhat irrelevant, as the relationships become the focus.

After a ten-year stint in Malawi as missionaries, John and Angie Wilmot moved to the town of Newman in the arid northwest of Western Australia, a town of contrasts with wealthy mining families and struggling indigenous folk. John and Angie have put down their roots among the Martu Aboriginal people, and have planted a church with them. The church is unable to pay for their needs, so they operate a funeral business across much of the northwest region. While the business has proved to be profitable enough to enable them to be self-sustaining, it also has the effect of frequently placing them in the lives of the indigenous people they minister to at the most difficult of times.

By contrast, Derek Gerrard is an entrepreneur who has operated successfully in business. He has generated sufficient income from his ventures to provide for his needs, while also pastoring a suburban church. He allocates one day of the working week to church activities as well as what is required on Sundays. Other than that, he operates in the business space and spends most of his energies there.[5]

Another businessman, but in a totally different context, is Genesis Efondo, a café owner and pastor on the small Philippine island of Virac. I met Genesis and his family over thirty years ago on a surfing trip to their island. His father was a pastor who lived off earnings from his tricycle work and his small peanut butter manufacturing operation. Genesis was only 6 years old when we visited, but a few years back he found me on Facebook and we reconnected. He told that he was now the pastor as his father had passed away and he was also a coffee roaster and café owner, and this was where he derived his income. While those of us in the western world may have a choice as to whether we are bivocational, in many parts of the world churches simply don't have the funds to even consider hiring a part-time pastor, let alone one who is employed *fully* by them.

I have given several examples of those who have been able to make the bivocational life work though, by and large, it is still perceived as a 'second best' option. It seems that most pastors would prefer to be working full time in the church, however I imagine they would find it hard to convince the apostle Paul that this was the most effective way to engage in ministry.

BUT WHY WOULD YOU? PAUL'S REASONS FOR TENTMAKING

While it's not unusual for the 'tentmaker' approach to be seen as an ideal way to enter foreign countries as missionaries, or for pastors in poorer nations, it seems to have less appeal in an affluent society where full-time church employment is possible and often expected. When we delve into Paul's approach to work and mission, we read in Acts 18 of his ability to take his trade on the road with him as he travelled:

> Paul left Athens and went to Corinth. There he met a Jew named Aquila, a native of Pontus, who had recently come from Italy with his wife Priscilla because Claudius had ordered all Jews to leave Rome. Paul went to see them, and because he was a tentmaker as they were, he stayed and worked with them.

Aquila and Priscilla were already living in Corinth and working as tent-makers while leading a church in their home. Upon hearing of Paul's arrival – whose reputation would have preceded him – they offered him a room as well as some casual employment. It was a win-win. Paul's self-funded approach to mission was a key element in his missionary strategy, and there are several reasons why Paul may have chosen this approach.

CREDIBILITY

From a background in Pharisaism and as a persecutor of Christians, any perception of mixed motives may have caused people to be hesitant about his message. So he intended to ensure that nothing stood in the way of the gospel. In 2 Corinthians 11, Paul compares himself to other so-called 'super-apostles' and states that he sought to never be a burden to the

Corinthians so that nothing would stand in the way of his message. It is interesting that in this letter Paul also wrote of accepting funds from the poverty-stricken church in Macedonia. Thus it would be wrong to see him as exclusively self-funded and opposed to any external support.

POSITIONING

Many of those early Christians came largely from the lower classes and the slaves who undertook manual labour; so perhaps Paul's tentmaking was a way to intentionally place himself amongst those who were coming to faith.[6] He would have been aware of the significance of his social environment and the strategic importance of being close to those among whom the gospel was taking root.

It seems Paul did not seek to operate a larger business with several employees, but rather one that functioned more like a sole trader. I suspect this simple, flexible approach to business was critical to allowing Paul the capacity to move around and serve the churches in different regions. Had he sought to establish a more substantial entity, he would have found himself busy with the administrative oversight tasks and his capacity for missionary work would have diminished.

VISIBILITY

Nothing places you in the hub of your community quite like running a small business, and nothing puts your ethics, integrity and love for people on display as much as your business interactions. As Paul constructed tents, those in the vicinity of his workspace would have observed his work ethic, his punctuality, and his treatment of other staff. They would have seen his commitment to producing quality tents, and they would have observed had he not chosen to take any short cuts in their production. Paul was either the 'real deal' and his message of the kingdom of God was present here as well as in the synagogue, or he was a fraud, a duplicitous person who spoke of one way of being but lived a completely different way in a non-religious context. No doubt when Paul stood up to speak in the synagogue, those who engaged with him in the marketplace observed him carefully and scrutinised his words.

FREEDOM

It seems likely that part of the reason Paul chose to sometimes not receive support from the churches is that he didn't want to be controlled by them. Once someone controls your income they have significant power in your life. And if you choose to speak in a way that brings offence to those with that power, then you may find yourself losing funds and possibly even a job. When the pastor is not solely dependent on the church for income, there is greater freedom to speak prophetically, to call for and lead difficult changes, and to bring rebuke should the need arise.

Paul's letters do not hold back from the truth he felt needed to be told. His security was definitely not connected to his financial situation. That's not to say he wasn't careful with money, or that he didn't need it. Rather, financial advancement wasn't the primary focus of his endeavours. Neither was it a non-issue; a business that doesn't make money won't survive long, and any ministry it supports will flounder.

FUNDING

If the churches were able to offer ongoing support to Paul and his team, then chances are it would have been a meagre amount. It certainly would not have provided for all of their needs. By contrast, as a businessperson, Paul could generate income to fund his missionary calling. Today many tentmaking jobs pay better than pastoral work, meaning that sometimes a pastor may not actually need the income from the church to make ends meet.

FLEXIBILITY

As a tentmaker, Paul worked in a 'portable' trade. He could travel from town to town and find work as he needed to. This would have been integral to helping fund his various missionary trips. It's not to say he sought out tentmakers in every place he visited, but there was often the opportunity for extra income if it was needed. Paul would also have been able to work for a sustained period, before taking time off to devote to missionary ventures.

In 2021, as we neared the end of our long service leave, we stopped for two nights at Eighty Mile Beach, an idyllic campground in the far north of our state. In the caravan across from our site was a new retiree, a man who had just sold his mobile caravan weighing business. I had no idea that such a service even existed. However, thirty minutes later after gently picking his brains, I headed back into the van and began googling 'mobile caravan scales'. While the irrigation business is fantastic, I was wondering:

a) how I could transition into something a little easier on the body;
b) if I could find a business activity that would allow us to travel to rural churches and serve them without the need for payment; and/or
c) if I could establish a small business that could support future church planters.

A few weeks later I had ordered a set of scales and established a new business which has slowly been gaining steam locally. It would be a simple matter to pack the scales in the back of the car as we travel, and to offer the service to the thousands of caravanners who are also on the road. This could be our self-supporting way of working among churches who may be struggling to afford a pastor.[7] I imagine Paul operated in this way with his tentmaking.

EXAMPLE

In 2 Thessalonians 3:6-8, Paul wrote a rebuke to a church where some were lazy and choosing not to work. Therefore, by engaging in his tentmaking trade, Paul offered an example of how they could provide for themselves and their families. If he had insisted on support from the church he may have appeared to be taking an easy path. Instead, his choice to make tents meant that no one could make this accusation. In fact, they were confronted with a man who worked hard during the day and served the church community 'after hours'.

GENEROSITY

It would be a mistake to think that Paul's decision to make tents was simply about providing for his own needs. Rather, part of his income was generated to take care of those he knew were in need. In Acts 20:33-35 he wrote:

> *I have not coveted anyone's silver or gold or clothing. You yourselves know that these hands of mine have supplied my own needs and the needs of my companions. In everything I did, I showed you that by this kind of hard work we must help the weak, remembering the words the Lord Jesus himself said: 'It is more blessed to give than to receive'.*

Paul's words suggest that his business was profitable enough to not only cater for his immediate needs and travel expenses, but also to assist the poor. Being both self-supporting and generous with his wealth would have ensured others listened to Paul and took him seriously. Similarly, as a result of his successful business ventures, Perth pastor and entrepreneur Derek Gerrard (mentioned previously) has established a charity to inspire everyday philanthropy (Meridian Global) and to give back both locally and further afield. At a personal level, he speaks of structuring his family finances in such a way that he lives off one third, invests one third, and gives one third away.[8] While Gerrard continues to lead a church, he is also able to generate income to serve the broader work of the kingdom.

IT'S OK TO RECEIVE SUPPORT TOO

In considering the way Paul went about his ministry, it's important to remember that he was not averse to receiving financial support from churches. In writing to the Philippian church, he spoke of gifts received at a time when he was in need.[9] As mentioned previously (2 Corinthians 11:8) Paul wrote of having 'robbed' other churches by receiving support from them to serve the Corinthians. He then wrote to the brothers in Macedonia who came and supplied his financial needs.

While Paul intentionally chose to limit his income from the churches he worked amongst, he did not argue that this was necessarily to be a model for others. He wrote to Timothy, explicitly stating that a worker is worthy of his wages,[10] and he told the Corinthians that those who preach the gospel should receive their living from the gospel. To the Galatians, he wrote that 'anyone who receives instruction in the word must share all good things with his instructor'.[11] Paul had no hesitation in building a case for those working in ministry being compensated for their time.

While he was not opposed to churches supporting those who have given time to oversight and leadership, it is highly doubtful that he had anything like our current 'professionalisation' in mind. My hunch is that when he wrote this, some were discovering a unique gifting and calling to lead and serve these new Christian communities, but to do so effectively meant time away from their professions. Eventually, there comes a tipping point where 'volunteering' time is no longer effective and a person needs to be freed up and supported to pursue a calling that has been affirmed by the rest of the community.

Paul's choice to make tents was not based on any kind of misplaced pride, or an inability to receive help from others. We can safely conclude that Paul both received support and earned enough to pay his way at other times.

Given Paul's lifestyle and the mobile nature of his trade, it's likely he worked when he needed to, or when he was settled in a town. When he was travelling or staying somewhere for only a short time, however, he may have accepted gifts and hospitality from others.

Author, Mark Russell suggests Paul would have accepted a variety of gifts for the following reasons:

- **To carry funds to people in need** – Paul was 'eager to remember the poor' (Galatians 2:10) and it would seem he made a point of gathering support, not for himself, but for those in need (1 Corinthians 16:1-3).
- **Travel expenses** – In ending the book of Romans, Paul mentioned Phoebe and commended her to them, as she was most likely the person to deliver the letter. Paul asked the Romans to give her any help she may need (Romans 16:2).

- **Establishment costs** – As many transient pastors will be aware, to move house is to incur costs. It may well be that lump sum gifts were given to help with this kind of event.
- **Road expenses** – Paul travelled a lot and sometimes he only stayed in places for a short time, meaning he was less likely to set up a business and seek out customers. These kinds of short-term trips would have benefited from Paul's presence, and the use of a gift may have allowed him to have a substantial ministry without having to source work.
- **General ministry costs** – In Ephesus, Paul held daily lectures in the hall owned by Tyrannus. It's likely he paid a substantial sum of money for this and he may have funded it from gifts and support he received.[12]

On several occasions Paul accepted hospitality from others (for example, Jason in Thessalonica – Acts 17:5-9) and this would be another way in which he was supported.

The choice to receive or decline support alongside any income from a workplace needs to be carefully thought through, with the consequences of each decision owned fully. If support comes with strings attached, then chances are it isn't the kind of support that any of us should be seeking. A wealthy tentmaker also needs to be careful not to behave arrogantly, as if they are above reproach because they are not reliant on the church's finances.

Perhaps a question worth considering is whether a pastor or missionary should continue to receive financial support if they can provide for their own needs out of their tentmaking income. I don't think there is one simple answer to this question. Rather, it depends on pastors discerning how the Spirit may be guiding them. During our time working as suburban missionaries, Danelle and I raised our income via personal support for several years. As the business flourished we ended up writing to our supporters, advising them that our needs had changed and we no longer required their funds. However, while working in the local church more recently, we have chosen to accept support, even though our business could fully fund the life we lead. The decision has been based on the recognition that we are devoting at least three days per week to what we do within the church, and foregoing potential business earnings during that time. There is also something about the presence of finances that calls for accountability and continued diligence on days and weeks where, as a volunteer, it may be possible to be lazy or to allocate time elsewhere.

INCARNATION LOOKS LIKE THIS

Paul was no stranger to hard work. He was willing to 'labour and toil night and day' to earn his money, and this strong work ethic would have boded well for the reception of his message.[13] In 2003 we had just begun planting a church in the new Perth suburb of Butler. At the time, I was working in three very flexible roles that allowed me to be available and accessible during the day. I hoped that by creating space in my life I would be able to use the time to connect with the men around me. It seemed like a good idea in principle, but it didn't work so well in practice.

Firstly, most of the men were at work during the day when I was free. Secondly, I discovered that at least one of those I spent time with ended up resenting me because I lived an apparently slow-paced, non-demanding and self-indulgent life while he worked hard in an unenjoyable factory job. In freeing myself from the regular workspace to be more available to people I had inadvertently created an obstacle to relationships. I was perceived as an outsider who didn't understand the world of hard labour. Had I chosen to work in similar roles to those in my community, I may have been more easily regarded as one of them.

It's not surprising then that I haven't had that accusation thrown at me since I started my irrigation business. In fact, the opposite is often true. Occasionally church people come work with me for a day or two and they discover how physically demanding my job can be. So there is no recipe for this approach to ministry, but rather a realisation of the varying needs in different contexts.

The bottom line of this discussion is the often tetchy issue of money, and what is needed to sustain oneself in life and ministry. Each person's perception of that will differ, and our individual contexts will also influence what we determine to be 'enough'. Some will have mortgages, while others will own homes. Some will send their children to private schools, while others go public. Some churches will pay generous wages, and others will pay the bare minimum. But there is no avoiding the reality that we need to earn money to survive in this world, and life is generally more enjoyable if we are not constantly worried about finances.

WHEREVER YOU GO THERE YOU ARE

I hadn't been in business long when I realised that I was having opportunities to speak of Jesus in ways that I had not experienced previously as a pastor. In this setting I was not a 'religious dude'; I was just the sprinkler repair guy who happened to believe in 'Jesus, Christianity and all that stuff'.

Instead of seeing the dual focus as a distraction from the main business of ministry, perhaps it is far healthier to see all of life as spiritual, and also to see our workplace as a fully funded mission opportunity. This applies to all forms of regular employment, whether it's a business, a professional role, or trade/labouring work. If mission is 'being sent' then surely we can be sent into a workspace where we can sensitively and creatively be the presence of Christ.

Rather than seeing tentmakers as those who head overseas and need a 'cover' for mission work, or seeing it as the last resort if a church is running short of funds, I believe all pastors should be seriously considering a dual-income stream as a possible direction that Christian ministry may take in future years.

As the COVID-19 pandemic began to impact the world in early 2020, churches were forced to close their doors on Sundays to minimise the risk of infection. Many members of the community lost jobs, or suffered a significant decrease in working hours, and it was clear that this was going to impact the local church's financial base. Subsequently, within a matter of days, a number of local pastors chose to decrease their working hours and to share the impact of the virus rather than expecting their congregation to keep contributing at the same rate. This was commendable leadership, but it raised the question: 'what else do you do when the tools in your kitbag have only equipped you to lead churches and preach sermons?' Perhaps a trade or profession attained before ministry would have prepared these folks for other options. Maybe those already equipped are returning to their trades and professions, and will discover a level of engagement with local people that they never thought possible while solely pastoring a church.

FOR REFLECTION

- Which of Paul's reasons for being a tentmaker resonate with you?
- What do you imagine Paul found hard about being a tentmaker? What is difficult for you?
- What joy do you imagine Paul experienced in his tentmaking?
- What are the high points of your own tentmaking experience?

- As a tentmaker, how would you discern when to accept funding and when to reject it?
- How do you feel when it comes to trusting God to provide financially? How may this impact your capacity for tentmaking?

Notes

1. Luke 8:1-3
2. Tertullian, *"Constitutions of the Holy Apostles"* II: LIX, in The Ante-Nicene Fathers, Vol. 7, Alexander Roberts and James Donaldson, eds. (Grand Rapids: Eerdmans Publishing Co., 1975), p. 424.
3. Guder, D., *The Missional Church*. Eerdmans Grand Rapids 1998 p. 191
4. Lai, Patrick (2012-02-04T22:58:59), *Tentmaking*. InterVarsity Press. Kindle Edition.
5. https://soundcloud.com/askalyka/derek-gerrard-entrepreneur-tech-investor-and-philanthropist-episode-9
6. Interview with Scot McKnight re Romans – https://vimeo.com/404338155 accessed 31.4.2021
7. www.weighmycaravan.com.au
8. https://soundcloud.com/askalyka/derek-gerrard-entrepreneur-tech-investor-and-philanthropist-episode-9
9. Phil 4:16-17
10. 1 Tim 5:18
11. Gal 6:6
12. Russell, L. M., *The Missional Entrepreneur*. (New Hope 2010) pp. 98-102
13. 2Thessalonians 3:8

6

WHO AM I AGAIN? VOCATION, CALLING & IDENTITY

As a teenager I was deeply inspired by the movie *Chariots of Fire* and the conviction shown by Eric Liddell, the brilliant Scottish athlete who refused to run in the heats of the Olympic 100m sprint because they were held on a Sunday. Liddell was criticised by many of his countrymen for this conscience decision, but he refused to bend. He later won gold in the 400 metre final. He is the man credited with turning the 400 metres from a middle-distance event into a sprint simply because he knew no other way to run.

As well as criticism from his country for his failure to run in the 100 metres, Liddell also endured critique from his family who hoped he would give his running away and become a missionary in China. However, Liddell had a bigger view of the world and of God than did those around him. While those close to him wanted him to go overseas and 'do God's work', Liddell realised that 'God's work' was right in front of him, doing what he had been uniquely equipped to do. There is a beautiful line in the film where Liddell responds to a challenge from his sister, Jenny, to give up his running. He says: "Jenny, God made me for a purpose, but he also made me *fast*, and when I run I feel his pleasure".

While Liddell inspired many with his athletic ability and his integrity of faith, perhaps what was missed was the fact that he was very much in touch with his sense of vocation – with exactly who God had created him to be. He knew that he was more alive when he was running than at any other time. In those moments, when he was sprinting, he was *feeling God's pleasure*. He was in tune with his calling and as a result his life aligned with that sense of identity.

If we are going to come to grips with the idea of living bivocationally then we must delve deeper into what we mean by the word 'vocation'.

When a school has a subject called 'Vocational Education' it is generally trying to help students discover the career path best suited to them – the mature version of asking a child: "What do you want to be when you grow up?" However, vocation has become so entangled with the notion of employment that it has been drained of its original vigour and beauty.

WHAT DO WE MEAN BY 'VOCATION'?

The word 'vocation' is derived from the Latin 'vocare' meaning 'calling', which gives us a dramatically different perception of what vocation might be. If I speak of having found my 'true calling', I may not necessarily be speaking of a religious endeavour. I could be a hairdresser, an auto mechanic or a bee-keeper, but the meaning of the phrase in this context is that I will have landed in my sweet spot by finding a job that suits me, and that I love.

In Christian circles 'calling' is also a word we need to use carefully, as it has significant connotations. Pastors will say they are 'called' to ministry by God and the accreditation or ordination committee (depending on your denomination) will ask a candidate to speak of their sense of 'calling' before being willing to approve them. 'Calling' is seen as an integral part of working in Christian leadership and, unless you can articulate a definite sense of call, it's unlikely a church will want to employ you in a pastoral role.

Os Guiness notes: 'there is no calling without a caller'.[1] To be called, we must be hearing the call from somewhere. When a secular society refers to our calling, it is speaking of us finding a direction and focus in life that aligns with our gifts, talents and personality. The Christian perspective taps into these dimensions, but is primarily derived from a relationship with the creator who interacts with us and guides our paths. Our vocation then speaks to both understanding and coming to grips with who God has created us to be.

Hugh Weschel writes of the source and nature of calling, distinguishing it clearly from the various 'jobs' we may have:

> *Vocational calling is the call to God and to his service in the vocational sphere of life, based on giftedness, desires, affirmations and human need. Vocation rightly understood transcends any given job, and our vocational calling – what God calls us to do based on our gifts, desires and the needs around us – can manifest in several different discrete jobs.*[2]

Up until the Reformation era, 'vocation' was a word that applied only to the religious careers in society, but Martin Luther was instrumental in recalibrating thinking around this subject. He argued that, because all of life was sacred, we could be serving God when milking a cow every bit as much as when praying for a sick child. It is from the Reformation era that what we know as the 'doctrine of vocation' emerges. Schurmann explains this:

> *According to this doctrine all relational spheres – domestic, economic, political, cultural – are religiously and morally meaningful as divinely given avenues through which persons respond obediently to the call of God to serve their neighbour in love.*[3]

In the Reformers' thinking, we are called to four spheres of influence in the world, with the implication that we have multiple vocations. Those areas are marriage and family, church, civic and career; and each vocation is imbued with significance as we enter them.

Schurmann explores the idea of vocation biblically and suggests that it has two significant meanings, or what we might call a primary and secondary calling.

Our primary call is to become a member of the people of God, and to take up the duties pertaining to that membership. The second meaning is God's diverse and particular calling – special tasks, offices or places of responsibility within the covenant community, and in the broader society. The words 'general' and 'particular' are sometimes used in place of 'primary' and 'secondary' to denote the two types of callings.

PRIMARY AND SECONDARY CALLINGS

In 2003, I encountered these two different strains of calling during our church planting venture. As a team, we wanted to purposely rethink church and mission from the ground up, and I was excited about what might eventuate.

Before arriving in our new neighbourhood I feverishly read every available book on mission and church planting. I wanted to better understand what it meant to be missionaries to the Western world. My wife, Danelle, wasn't doing her reading though, and I was worried. I knew she wasn't reading because *Church Planting* by Stuart Murray Williams had sat on her bedside table for over two months with the bookmark in the same place.

Disappointing.

I had given her the book as a primer, to inspire her and help her understand the theology and practice around incarnational mission. It was essential reading in my opinion.

So I asked her: "Are you sure you know what we are going to do when we hit the ground in Brighton?"

"Yeah, I think so," she answered confidently, but without elaborating.

I wasn't convinced she knew the heart of our mission and what we were about, but neither did I want to question her confidence. I asked this same question once more and got the same reply. A smarter man would have left it there and moved on. I, however, had to ask yet again: "Honey, I know I've asked this before, but can you just tell me if you're sure you are confident in what we are doing here?"

Without blinking she looked me in the eye. "Yeah, I think I've got it. You want us to love God and love others. That's it, hey?"

I was flummoxed. She was right. That was exactly what we were going to do and, while she hadn't couched it in the same terms I may have, her interpretation was correct. I left the conversation with my tail between my legs and a 'note to self' that when your wife says she's 'got it' then she's probably 'got it'.

On reflection I now realise she was articulating her *primary* calling, (which was also mine), but I was asking if she had grasped our more *particular* calling for that time – to be suburban missionaries, to deconstruct our long years of church experience, and to rebuild from the ground up. I wanted to know if she was hoping we would hire a building and invite people to come, or if she had understood our focus on mission first and church second. It turns out she was in tune with all of that intuitively, but the answer she gave spoke to the question of 'primary calling' while I was actually asking a question about 'secondary calling'.

The Bible is clear about our primary calling – to live in a relationship with the creator and to participate in his redemptive purposes within the world. From Abraham and Moses, to Peter and John, to you and I today, we have each experienced the call of God, who has adopted us into his family and made us children of God.[4] Not all would agree that God 'calls' us to secondary vocations; some see these activities more as a function of spiritual gifts, personal preferences and life situations.

FLUIDITY IN CALLING

Miroslav Volf is one person who writes of becoming increasingly dissatisfied with the vocational understanding of work, inherited from the Reformers and predominant in Christian circles. In the preface to *Work in the Spirit* he challenges these long held views:

> *The vocational understanding of work was developed and refined in the context of fairly static feudalist and early capitalist societies on the basis of a static theological concept of vocation. Modern societies, however, are dynamic. A single, permanent, salaried and full-time form of employment has given way to multiple and frequently changing jobs. Such a dynamic society requires a dynamic understanding of work. It was clear to me that the dead hand of 'vocation' needed to be lifted from the Christian idea of work. It is both inapplicable to modern societies and theologically inadequate.*[5]

Volf proposes that the concept of 'charisma' should become the cornerstone of a new and fresh understanding of work and vocation, and then develops what he calls a pneumatological and eschatological framing of this issue. Essentially Volf argues that our vocation should be fluid rather than static, and a reflection of how the spirit has gifted us. In his view, as we live out our vocation on this Earth, we will both contribute to, and point to, the ultimate new creation.

While Volf's work resonates with a modern, more transient culture, there is definitely biblical precedent for conceiving of 'particular' callings. In Acts 6, as the church began to grow and their food distribution project encountered teething problems, the apostles paused, prayed, and then appointed seven men to give oversight to this initiative. In this sense, they were given a particular vocation. In Ephesians 2:10, we are described as God's handiwork – his *poema* – created in Christ to do good works, which God prepared in advance for us to do. God has already envisioned the areas in which our lives will be invested and, as we listen to Him, we can discern and move into those callings. In Acts 13, as the church prayed, the Spirit spoke, asking specifically for Paul and Barnabas to be set aside for future missionary work. In that moment, there was a clear sense of God's unique and particular call to both the church and to them.

Around the time of writing this book, my son, Sam, was finishing his final year of school, considering his future, and trying to discern a sense of calling. 'Where may God want me to go from here?' was the question he was pondering. Together we talked and prayed, we looked at his various capacities, the orientation of his heart and his hopes for the future. We considered job opportunities, the kind of life that accompanies various careers, and how faith may be expressed in different work environments. In those conversations, we were seeking to help him discern what his calling may look like – how God may direct him in line with who He has made him to be. There is an awareness that this is an unfolding story and that, as Volf argues, there may be multiple callings at different points in life.

IMPERSONATING OURSELVES OR BECOMING OURSELVES?

In his book, *Let Your Life Speak*, Parker Palmer writes of 'becoming himself', of the call coming from within as he learnt who he was, and how he moved towards being his true self. He writes: 'I was indeed wearing other people's faces and I can tell you exactly who they were'. He takes the view that vocation is less related to employment or career and more derived from an innate sense of identity that forms as we mature. He writes of his previous view of vocation as duty and then says:

> *Today I understand vocation quite differently – not as a goal to be achieved, but as a gift to be received. Discovering vocation does not mean scrambling toward some prize just beyond my reach but accepting the treasure of true self I already possess. Vocation does not come from a voice 'out there' calling me to become something I am not. It comes from a voice 'in here' calling me to be the person I was born to be, to fulfill the original selfhood given me at birth by God.*[6]

What does it look like to 'become ourselves'? Back in the mid 90s I attended the National Youth Workers Convention in San Diego and listened to Mike Yaconelli speak in impassioned tones: "Youth pastors – we have to stop impersonating ourselves!" I didn't know what he meant. I was utterly puzzled by this statement for five or six years until it dawned on me that he was simply saying we must be careful not to form ourselves into the ideal youth worker we have in our imagination. Rather, we should be true to the kind of youth worker God has created us to be. To my chagrin, I realised then that I hadn't understood this before because I *had* been impersonating myself. I had been a caricature of who I was called to be, instead of allowing myself to be formed by the Spirit into the kind of youth pastor I was created to be.

Perhaps my son, Sam, just needs to listen to the 'voice inside', but I'd suggest that's a difficult thing for even a mature, adult Christian to do. There is always noise from parental expectations, personal ambitions, and societal pressure influencing and calling us each to their preferred path. How will Sam hear the voice of God amid the cacophony? And this is a seventeen-year-old with few financial responsibilities to consider! He can probably 'follow his dreams' at this point in his life as he will be purely self-supporting, and can live on beans for weeks on end if the need arises. But should he get married, have children, and buy a home, the ability to discern vocation becomes more complex. It is now being heard in muffled tones, filtered through the demands of a typical Western lifestyle. Perhaps this is why younger people seem to more readily hear the call of God to audacious adventures.

BEWARE OF VOCATIONAL DISTORTIONS

Guinness writes insightfully of two errors we are prone to when it comes to understanding vocation. He calls these the Catholic distortion, and the Protestant distortion.

Of the Catholic distortion he writes:

> *The truth of calling means that for followers of Christ, 'everyone, everywhere, and in everything' lives the whole of life as a response to God's call. Yet this holistic character of calling has often been distorted to become a form*

> *of dualism that elevates the spiritual at the expense of the secular. This distortion may be called the 'Catholic distortion' because it rose in the Catholic era and is the majority position in the Catholic tradition.*[7]

The idea that there is a higher calling in the spiritual realm is the distortion Guinness speaks of. He cites early church historian, Eusebius, as one of the earliest advocates for this cause, who writes of the 'perfect life' of contemplation reserved for priests, nuns and those with this so called higher calling, in contrast to the 'permitted life' for those not 'called' and who are required to work in ordinary jobs.

On the other hand, the Protestant distortion focuses on the secular but in an equally misleading way.

> *Under the pressure of the modern world, the Protestant distortion is more extreme. It severs the secular from the spiritual altogether and reduces vocation to an alternative word for work. In so doing, it completely betrays the purpose of calling and, ironically, activates a counter-reaction that swings back to the Catholic distortion again. Better, it would seem, the dualism of making calling purely spiritual than the dualism of making calling purely secular.*[8]

Amongst the Reformers, Luther saw that Christians answer the call of God by choosing a job in alignment with their faith, while Calvin was quicker to make calling and workplace synonymous. In time, the Puritans who followed began to use words such as trade, job and occupation interchangeably with calling and vocation, until eventually the connection between a person's faith and their workplace was lost entirely.

Vocation has been clothed in many different ways by various schools of theologians but, at its core, it still speaks to a sense of calling – either an inner voice that is the Spirit of God or an outer voice (family/mentors/friends) that we attend to – perhaps also the Spirit of God. What is less clear is whether we can legitimately speak of being *bivocational*, or whether we are actually 'mono-vocational' but with the possibility that our vocation is expressed in a multitude of ways. Kueker would argue this is the case:

> *A Christian who engages in a money-earning profession such as making tents, to support a non-money-earning profession such as teaching about Jesus, would be more accurately described as 'dual service' rather than 'bivocational' – one calling, two forms of service. The same would be true of any Christian who serves in more than one line of work.*[9]

Conversely, Cahalan would argue that we have multiple vocations dependent on our stage of life. While we tend to associate the discernment of vocation primarily with young adulthood, Cahalan suggests that vocations are also present for the elderly and at other stages of life, thus seeing vocation as flexible and transitory rather than singular and constant.[10]

My own experience suggests that vocation is sensed in younger years, gains clarity in younger adulthood and sharpens further in middle age. At fifty-seven years old I sense my vocation deeply and can articulate it more clearly than at any other stage in life. I resonate with Parker Palmer's notion of 'becoming myself' as I feel less pressure to conform to other people's ideas of who I ought to be. I identify deeply with Paul's voice of being called to be a missionary; however, I also sense a calling to use my communication skills both inside and beyond the church. The fact that I can generate income by doing something I enjoy (irrigation and landscaping) is a blessing, but I feel as though I could easily engage in other types of business and still support my primary focus. By contrast, my father is eighty-seven and less clear on what his vocation is now that he is no longer as fit and active as he once was. This possible deterioration of vocation is a concern for the elderly, and others no longer able to function as they once did. It can be a source of frustration and anxiety as they question their worth in the world.

BI, CO, MONO, TRANS – DOES IT MATTER?

So which is it? Do we have one vocation but multiple outworkings as Kueker suggests, or is there such a status as genuinely 'bivocational'?

As part of a class on mission, NSW theology professor, Ian Robinson, recorded ten audio interviews with different pastors asking them to reflect on their bivocational roles. In each interview he asked the question: "What do you think of the word 'bivocational' as distinct from the more traditional 'tentmaker'?"[11]

In response, New Zealand theology professor and pastor, Steve Taylor, was quick to state that he doesn't like either term, although he doesn't have a better suggestion. Steve also said he has never seen himself as bivocational, but rather that he was called to a life of teaching, and ministry, and service, and that he was expressing that calling in different contexts. He pushed back on the term 'tentmaking' because he felt it implied that he was doing a job by necessity, in order to allow him to do ministry related work.

Similarly, Geoff Hurst, a Uniting Church pastor who served for many years in the remote regions of North-Western Australia, did not regard himself as having two vocations. During his time pastoring the Karratha

Uniting Church, he saw the need for the town to have better internet service. With his background in information technology, he set about starting a small Internet Service Provider (ISP). On reflection, Geoff did not see his business dealings as another unique vocation. He described himself as an 'opportunist', who saw a gap in the market that aligned with his experience and skills, a gap that also allowed him to serve his community in a much-needed way. So he took a risk and started a new enterprise. Despite spending long hours running this service to meet the needs of the local people, his sense of vocation was actually to be a pastor to the people of the town. His business enabled him to meet with, and enter the homes of many, who would not want anything to do with a church. In that way, he could 'pastor' and care for them as needs arose.

I had forgotten I had taken part in this series of interviews, so I listened to my contribution with curiosity. When asked how I felt about the word 'bivocational', I replied that I didn't care; the word was irrelevant and I was more concerned with getting on with the job of mission and ministry. It was a thoroughly pragmatic response; however I have since sought to think more deeply about this idea. Now I *do* care because I believe the language we use matters and forms our thinking about the subject.

Most pastors would argue that their primary vocation is to serve the mission of God amongst both the church and the wider community. They may also use other means to make ends meet, but these will usually be 'jobs' that may or may not be vocationally aligned. It seems more common to find part-time pastors working in other ministry and people-related roles, rather than in professional jobs or trades work. This makes sense, as there is a degree of synergy and complementarity about the roles, rather than having to learn and practice a completely new set of skills.

When writing about the idea of being bivocational Hugh Halter takes a different angle:

> *We use the term bivocational to simply mean those who learn to blend two primary callings. The first is to work to provide for ourselves and our family.*[12]

He goes on to cite 2 Thessalonians 3:6-10 where Paul writes about providing for our own needs through work rather than being idle and a burden to others. Halter then states:

> *The second is to see our entire lives leveraged and in use for God's kingdom purposes, to live intentionally as a missionary saint. I believe every believer is called to these two callings or vocations or jobs if you will, and so a business owner, employee climbing the corporate ladder, stay at home mother, as well as anyone in a vocational ministry position share these callings.*[13]

Halter suggests there are two specific roles we occupy in society, that of 'worker' and that of Christ-follower. The 'leveraging' of our everyday life for Christ's purposes is also in line with a holistic, rather than dualistic approach to life.

Brad Brisco, who is the Director of Bivocational Church Planting for the North American Mission Board, has chosen to create the term 'covocational' to push back on the sacred/secular dualism that has complicated our thinking on this issue. He rightly argues:

> *All Christians are called to full-time ministry, doing good work well for the glory of God, regardless of their specific vocation. If God reigns over all things (and He does), then all things are sacred.*[14]

In his church planter's manual, he writes about why he has chosen to use the 'co' prefix rather than 'bi':

> *To help overcome this disconnection, I will often use the term covocation. The prefix co is the reduced form of the Latin com which means 'together' or 'in common'. English words like cofounder, copilot, coauthor or companion are examples of words that denote partnership and equality. Covocation embodies the reality that if a person is called to be a dentist, a teacher or a plumber, and at the same time is called to start a church, the different callings are not isolated from one another; instead, they are interlinked and equal. The language of covocation pushes against the temptation to compartmentalize different aspects of our lives.*[15]

Brisco suggests that a key distinction between a bivocational church planter and a co-vocational pastor is that the former will eventually hope to leave the workplace and focus fully on the church work, while the latter will intentionally remain fully invested in both areas simultaneously, and will not see the need for one to have priority. While Brisco's definitions do help to clarify different approaches to this form of ministry, I feel like the reality is more messy and fluid than the descriptors allow for.

As an example, my observation of Paul's life would suggest that he felt a deep and ongoing calling to be the 'apostle to the Gentiles', but this vocation was expressed in many different ways. At times he lived in a city and made tents while preaching in his spare time. On other occasions he seemed to pause for periods and invest significantly in the life of the church. Perhaps on these occasions he relied fully on the church for support. We simply don't find one specific bivocational model in scripture, but we see people who chose to pursue their calling from God, and adapted their modes of operation and sources of income to suit the context they found themselves in.

If our vocation emanates from our deepest sense of being then it is less likely to be tied to a specific profession or task, and more likely to be a reflection of who we perceive ourselves to be in the world. In a purely secular worldview, our vocation can only align with our passions, skills and opportunities. It is something we do or something we give ourselves to. But once we allow for the reality of God, we introduce another element that actually gives shape to all of our hopes, dreams and ambitions and, ultimately, to the way we choose to live our life.

A PROCESS FOR DISCOVERING VOCATION

In coaching and mentoring conversations, I have made it a practice to ask people what they feel they are here on Earth to do. In essence, how would they frame their sense of purpose and vocation? Often I will tell the story of Eric Liddell and his sense of feeling 'God's pleasure' when he was running. As people resonate with Liddell's language, I then ask them what activities they are engaged in when they experience God's pleasure.

For example, in my own life I experience God's pleasure when I am surfing – alone with the natural environment and connecting with him. In the work sphere; writing an article I feel passionate about, teaching the Bible creatively and inspiring people to follow Jesus, laying a new lawn for someone, being able to solve an irrigation problem others had been unable to resolve, are just some of the moments when I feel my heart soar and I feel like I am doing the very things for which I was created.

Not everyone can answer the question of vocation quickly or easily, but some can, and their answer generally has less to do with their actual work role, but (if they are Christians) more to do with their sense of identity in Christ and how that gets expressed in the world around them.

So how do you find clarity around vocation? How can anyone say with certainty that 'this is who I am called to be'?

My own experience has been a convergence of desire, gifting, opportunity, and spiritual intuition over many years. I can now say confidently that I am a missionary church leader who also runs a couple of businesses. I don't feel especially *called to* be an irrigation repairer. I have a knack for business and sense I could engage in any business activity (ethics permitting) that generated income, allowed for engagement with the world, and freed me to serve in a local church. In that sense, I am not bivocational. I have *one* clear vocation, but it is expressed in two very different settings.

If a person is genuinely seeking to discern God's calling in their life then the following may be helpful:

a) **Biblical reflection and listening to the Spirit** speaking through scripture. Not many have 'burning bush' moments, but it is possible that, in reading the biblical story, you may find a connection with your own journey.

b) **Personal reflection and journaling** that focuses on areas such as your spiritual gifts, inclinations, personality type, and significant achievements. Completing a personal inventory of how you are wired, and what you have been involved in up to this point, will be very helpful.

c) **Some form of discernment process with others** in the church community. Listening to others, we trust, will assist our own decision making. Their perception may also challenge and refine some of our misconceptions.

d) **Being aware of the Ignation ideas of consolation and desolation** may also guide us into paths where we are aligned with the

Spirit and his work, rather than other people's expectations of us or the 'path of least resistance'.[16]

e) **The simple action of practically 'trying' a pathway** to see if it is one we wish to walk down further is important. Those unsure of whether local church ministry is their future would be wise to serve voluntarily before committing to any longer training process.

As a caution, I want to warn against elevating the idea of calling to a form of mystical experience reserved for the privileged or the special. Could it be that in looking for biblical comparisons, such as a burning bush, we have marginalised the call experience of many people who feel destined for the ordinary devoid of the divine?

Is there a better word than bivocational? I'm not sure I can invent one and, even if I did, it has to be in popular use for it to have currency. I like Brad Brisco's 'covocational', but it also implies that a person has two vocations. Perhaps a person with more than one form of employment could be considered *transvocational* as they spread their energies across two distinct roles? At the end of the day, I resign myself to using a word I feel ill at ease with simply because it is recognised in common parlance. The language matters, but perhaps what matters more is tracking your life journey and experiences, and to be able to recognise the voice of God calling you and shaping you as you go.

My greatest hope would be that, as the next cohort of bivocational pastors approach their roles with vigour and joy, the language of being bivocational will no longer have a second best tinge to it. Instead it will be seen as the normal way to lead a church in a secular culture. The word 'bivocational' would no longer draw looks of pity, but the bivocational pastor would be esteemed by those around them for their conscious and purposeful choice to serve God in such a way. That will be a wonderful day!

FOR REFLECTION

- When you speak of your work, do you most often view it as a profession, a career, a job, or a vocation? How does this perception impact your approach to it?
- Of the various definitions and ideas for vocation listed above (Weschel, Schurmann, Volf, Palmer) which do you identify with most?
- How easily are you able to articulate your sense of vocation?
- Has your vocation shifted over the years, or has it stayed constant?
- Are you bivocational and, if so, what do *you* mean by that?
- Scottish Olympic runner, Eric Liddell, was known to have said: "When I run I feel His pleasure". What do you most feel God's pleasure doing?
- Where have you had to operate outside of your calling, and how does that affect you?
- What would be your most obvious spiritual gifts and natural capacities? How do these inform your calling?
- Can you recall specific 'God moments' where you were aware of His call in your life?
- If you are already bivocational, how would you describe your life to: a) a church member; and b) a neighbour?
- If you are bivocational, do you feel that one of your roles has priority over the other and, if so, why is that the case?

Notes

1. Guinness, Os, *The Call*. Thomas Nelson. Kindle Edition. Location 131 of 4496
2. https://tifwe.org/how-to-understand-your-vocational-calling/
3. Schurmann, Douglas. Vocation (Grand Rapids: Eerdmans 2004), p.4
4. Ephesians 1:4-5
5. Volf, Miroslav, *Work in The Spirit*. 2001 Wipf and Stock Eugene Oregon p vii preface
6. Palmer, Parker, *Let Your Life Speak: Listening for The Voice of Vocation*. (San Franciso: Jossey Bass 2000) p. 10
7. Guinness, Os, *The Call*. Thomas Nelson. Kindle Edition. Location 641 of 4496
8. Guinness, Os, *The Call*. Thomas Nelson. Kindle Edition. Location 649 of 4496
9. https://www.theologyofwork.org/new-testament/acts/a-clash-of-kingdoms-community-and-powerbrokers-acts-13-19/tent-making-and-christian-life-acts-181-4
10. Cahalan, Kathleen, *Calling All Years Good*. Wm. B. Eerdmans Publishing Co. Kindle Edition.
11. Ian Robinson – Bivocational Conversations 2017
12. Halter, Hugh, *Bivocational: A Modern-Day Guide for Bivocational Saints*. Missio Publishing. Kindle Edition. Loc 165 of 1524
13. Halter, Hugh, *Bivocational: A Modern-Day Guide for Bivocational Saints*. Missio Publishing. Kindle Edition. Loc 165 of 1524
14. Brisco, Brad, *Covocational Church Planting*. (SEND Network Alpharetta 2018) p.24
15. Brisco, Brad, *Covocational Church Planting*. (SEND Network Alpharetta 2018) p.24
16. https://jesuitschoolsnetwork.org/wp-content/uploads/2020/01/Consolation-and-Desolation_Revised.pdf Accessed 15.5.2021

7

JESUS HAD A REAL JOB

Early in our marriage, I was asked to hang the washing on the clothesline, so I headed out to the backyard with the basket of wet clothes. A short while later Danelle appeared and she was laughing.

"That's not how you hang clothes!"

"What do you mean? This is the way I have always done it. What's wrong with it?"

So began a rather pointless conversation about the right and wrong way to peg up T-shirts, socks and underwear. Thirty years later, she still does things her way and I do them my way – the wrong way! When all is said and done the aim is to get the clothes dry. Simple, right? And given there are no textbooks or formal training for optimal clothesline operations, surely there can be no correct or incorrect method.

The same is true when it comes to bivocational church leadership. There is no one biblical or right way to do it. What does matter is working and living in a way that is both purposeful and sustainable, that allows your church to be served and your non-church role to be performed well too.

While some approach the bivocational life as ordained ministers with a side hustle, others consider both vocational tasks as being equally weighted, in regards to calling and value, in the kingdom of God. The same God, who calls the full-time megachurch pastor, speaks to another person and calls them to be a plumber. While we ascribe status to each of these roles based on our societal and cultural estimation of them, there is no ranking in the kingdom of God. None whatsoever. There is no meaningless work, even if we choose to think of it that way. All of our work serves others in some way and, in doing so, we honour God. In this chapter we will seek to explore the various ways in which the bivocational life takes shape, the reasons we may wish to consider being bivocational, as well as some reasons that may sway us away from the bivocational life.

SNAPSHOTS OF THE BIVOCATIONAL LIFE

Some people are naturally gifted at thinking creatively and imagining possibilities. Others need a kick start to get the creative juices flowing. If you're in the latter category, then this next section is designed to help you envisage how you may be able to live and serve bivocationally.

Among those I surveyed for this book were teachers, journalists, web designers, mums, and many other people. Notably, there were virtually no blue-collar/trade workers. Many worked in roles that complemented ministry in some way or other (chaplains, denominational workers) but few worked in roles completely divorced from their ministry. All of my examples come from my own Australian context, but chances are you will have similar expressions taking shape in your backyard.

As previously mentioned, one striking image of the bivocational pastor was the 'worker pastors' of the late 1970s in Western Australia. At the time, the Baptists wanted to plant churches in the Pilbara and Kimberley regions of far North Western Australia. It was harsh, difficult territory, but rich with iron ore and various mineral deposits, meaning that towns were being established and communities were forming. Beginning with Port Hedland, then Karratha, Tom Price, and Newman, Baptist churches were established by those prepared to be *worker pastors,* men who went to those areas with their families and took up full-time jobs as teachers, or who found jobs in the mines and pastored when they were 'off duty'.

My in-laws, Peter and Val Faulkner, served for many years in this way, and remember it fondly as some of their richest ministry, but it was also extremely difficult to work thirty-eight hours in regular employment, and then to lead a church 'after hours', particularly in the stifling heat and extreme isolation of these towns. Rob Douglas was one of those worker pastors and was bivocational for all of his time in the North West. He served at churches in Derby, Roebourne and Carnarvon, while working as a journalist, car detailer, hospital cleaner, and supermarket shelf stacker. While ministry came at a cost to the worker pastors of the North West, it also happened organically, in the flow of life, as weekends were spent with the church family at the river or the gorges. In these smaller communities, many people were displaced from family, so the church filled that gap and became their family.

One of the survey questions I asked pastors was whether their 'secular' work was a choice or a necessity. Perhaps the easiest way to determine that is to take away the need for that income source, and see if they would still choose to be involved in the work. For most the answer is simple: they would quickly give away their second job if the church could pay the bills. For a few, however, it wasn't so clear.

Simon Elliot is the pastor at The Big Table, a church network that meets in homes in the south of Perth, but he also manages his own design and advertising business. On top of this, he is a running coach, a role in which his hobby overlaps with income generation and Christian mission. Being his own boss, Simon can manage time as he wishes and, after twenty-seven years of business, he is no longer working hard just to survive.

Another husband and wife pastoral team living in a large regional city also stated that they are bivocational by choice rather than by necessity. The professions in which they are employed provide excellent salaries and allow for greater financial independence and life choices, but their primary reason for staying in this mode is more to do with being connected to the community in which they serve.

As previously mentioned, Derek Gerrard planted and continues to lead a church in Scarborough, Western Australia. Derek devotes Thursdays and Sundays to church and other days to business pursuits. Interestingly, Derek would suggest he is primarily called to the business world where he has enjoyed success. He is unique in this way, as the overwhelming majority of pastors surveyed view local church planting or ministry as their primary calling, and their other role as subservient to this. I am unaware of any other pastors who intentionally engage in pastoring as a 'secondary' role.

Likewise, there are few pastoral team leaders whose other role is 'mum'. Caroline Meers in Woolongong City Church, New South Wales, has been in the senior pastoral leadership role for nine years now, after transitioning from a youth pastor position. She already had credibility with the church and, in a time of transition, she was appointed to the team leader role, which she has made her own, adjusting and tweaking as necessary. She is settled in this position, enjoys it, and her church is healthy.

Work Component	Church/ Mission Component	Description	Missional Effectiveness
Full-time work in profession or trade	As able	It's a tough place to be and is generally unsustainable if a typical understanding of the pastor's role is adhered to.	May be effective in job, but difficult to lead a church at the same time.
Part-time in a similar field – e.g. chaplain	Part-time	This can be a good fit because jobs align, or it may create a 'bubble' if the other job is in ministry with Christians.	It can work but missional component may be minimal.
Part-time – job that 'pays the bills'	Part-time	A 'subsistence' income. While it pays the bills, the 'other job' is often one that lacks enjoyment, challenge and opportunity, e.g. night fill.	Workable but not ideal as the work is likely uninspiring.
Part-time professional job	Part-time	This has several advantages with the pastor obviously having higher earning potential, as well not being bound by the church and its income.	A great option if you can find a professional job that allows for part timers.
Running a small business	Part-time	This has potential for great freedom and increased earnings, but a person needs to have a knack for business, or it could end in overwork and exhaustion.	Great potential if you are self disciplined and entrepreneurial.
Home duties – mum/dad	Part-time	Although these roles don't generate income, they allow for freedom and flexibility.	Excellent potential if you can use your role to foster connections.
Seasonal work	Seasonal ministry	This may be applicable in rural settings where farmers are more available at some times of the year than others.	Effective 'in season'.

These examples offer a small snapshot of what may be possible. This table is a summary of the major ways in which bivocational ministry can be expressed.

Ultimately whatever combination of employment and ministry you choose has to work for you. It has to be at *least* tolerable, hopefully meaningful, and preferably enjoyable. It also has to pay enough to enable you and your family to live. But our work does not have to be personally fulfilling for it to be important work. The Reformers pointed out that the first priority of our work was that it was of service to others. Enjoyment and gratification could be factored in after this.

There are occasions when our work may feel meaningless, or filled with drudgery, but it's possible that the meaning we ascribe to it is the real problem. Early in our marriage, Danelle and I spent an evening in Sydney en route to New Zealand. As we left the airport for a back-packer joint called The Funkhouse (not recommended) we began chatting to our taxi driver, who seemed remarkably energetic and friendly for 10.00 pm at night. He asked us about what we were doing and pointed out sites of interest. Upon reaching the hotel he said: "You know, I have the most important job in Sydney! When people come to this city I am the first person they meet, so I am their first impression of the city. I can make them welcome and excited to be here, or I can quietly drive them to the hotel and say nothing. I want them to feel like this is the greatest place on Earth to be. That's what I do!"

This guy nailed it. He was a cab driver – hardly the most exciting job on the planet at face value – but the meaning he attributed to his role converted the mundane into the significant. We can do this in our workplaces as we ask: "What does it mean to be the presence of Jesus in this context and this job?" As we attribute significance and meaning to our employment, we will work with a far greater sense of purpose.

10 REASONS WHY YOU MAY WISH TO BECOME BIVOCATIONAL

Why would you intentionally choose to spread your energies across two different areas of work, rather than just giving your all to one project? There are some legitimate reasons to do so, and some that are not so convincing. If you intend to head down this route then it's essential to assess your motivations and intentions. In chapter one we explored some of the big picture reasons for the church to move in this direction. Now it's time to explore some of the more immediate and personal benefits.

Reason 1: You See The Missional Potential

As I read about Paul's life, I have no doubt he saw the missional potency of being physically present in the business community, and of being in significant relationships with other people in the region. This reality only hit home personally as I began to manage my own business, and realised how quickly and easily I had become enmeshed in the community. Some full-time pastors have excellent community connections, but I also know that, for some, mission is another task to be completed when they escape the bubble that church so often becomes. For the person employed in their local community, mission becomes an integrated part of life.[1]

If you see the missional potential of connecting with your community through a job of some sort, then it is also worth considering what type of work will best serve your missionary endeavours. It's obvious that jobs requiring face-to-face contact enable a sharing of life in a more significant way, than running an online business will ever allow. So if you hope to release your missional energy, then begin by considering roles that will place you in close proximity to the people with whom you want to connect.

In the early days of my irrigation business, I found myself working for a client who pulled up a camping chair with a beer in his front porch and wanted to chat. As we got to know one another, he discovered I was a pastor and I heard him speak of his upcoming wedding.

"Who's doing the wedding for you?" I asked.

"We don't know yet. You don't do weddings do you?"

"Yeah I do as a matter of fact," I responded.

From there we spent some time in pre-marriage counseling before I conducted their wedding a little later that year. I still hear from him each time his sprinklers fail and he needs a hand, but it's always a conversation that is a little warmer than most because we have celebrated one of life's special moments together.

As well as the customer connection, there is the workplace networking that occurs. I have spent time helping several younger men establish their irrigation businesses and navigate the challenges that go with being a solo operator. As a person who has now been in business longer than most, I occasionally receive calls from competitors asking for my advice or thoughts on how they can complete a job. I have intentionally positioned myself to be generous in this way by sharing my expertise, and it has enabled a healthy network.

If you live with a missionary/ministry mindset then no matter what job you do you will see opportunity everywhere. What matters is simply being yourself and responding to the Spirit as He calls you to engage with different people at different times.

Reason 2: To Embrace A New Paradigm Of Ministry

There is no question that our understanding of what it means to be the church, and do ministry, has been shaped predominantly by the full-time pastoral model in the Christendom-based church. With this imagination come expectations that the pastor will perform certain duties.

Some of the more traditional expectations of a pastor are that he or she will:

- be available to church members around the clock;
- visit church members in their homes;
- take responsibility for a lion's share of Sunday morning duties;
- make sure all aspects of the church are functioning;
- fill the gaps when they appear, whether it's children's ministry, youth or cleaning duties; and
- be the servant of the church.

A part-time pastor can move out of the traditional paradigm, become less a general practitioner and more of a specialist, functioning in the area of their giftedness and strengths. This simple role shift can also catalyse a broader scale reimagining of mission and purpose within the whole church, and lead to significant change.

A bivocational pastor, who is freed of traditional expectations, may then be able to think creatively and innovatively about what shape church may take and what forms of ministry may connect with their local community.

Reason 3: Credibility

Some observe the pastoral life as privileged, a role where you largely set your own working hours and use your discretion to choose where to spend time.

Paul was aware that some may have viewed him as milking the church for funds simply to look out for himself. That's why, in 2 Corinthians 2:17, he wrote: 'Unlike so many, we do not peddle the word of God for profit. On the contrary, in Christ we speak before God with sincerity, as those sent from God.'

Clearly, there were (and still are) a number who identified ministry as a way to make money. Paul was adamant that he did not want to be categorised as one of them. By choosing the bivocational life, he hoped to make a statement about his commitment and integrity.

Reason 4: Job Sharing Works Better

The idea that one person has the capacity to bring all that is needed to help a church flourish is seriously flawed. While the single, full-time model may ensure the pastor is fully employed, even the most seemingly omnicompetent pastor has areas of weakness, and will need to devolve work to others.

Unpaid help has been the way church ministries have operated for many years; however, it would seem we are currently looking more and more to specialised paid staff for oversight of ministry areas, with volunteers merely assisting. It is now common for even smaller churches to have paid part-time children's workers, youth workers, and worship leaders. A downside to this approach is that volunteers may no longer be seen (by themselves or others) as ministers in their own right, but simply as helpers to the main 'minister' and this is problematic both theologically and practically.

Reason 5: You Want To Be Independent Of Your Church's finances

There are good reasons for not accepting funds from your church. These include alleviating any financial difficulty the church may be facing, freeing up funds for other staff members, or simply because you don't need the extra income. When a pastor chooses this path it is usually a noble gesture, and an indication of their desire for the church to flourish and not be under any burden. Occasionally the choice not to receive funds may be made from unhealthy reasons, such as being free from oversight or accountability.

By choosing not to take income from the church, you do run the risk of starting to perceive yourself as a volunteer, and cutting yourself some breaks that would never be given to a paid staff member. If, as you envisage taking this route, you see yourself skipping the meetings you dislike and taking weekends away whenever you feel like it, then you have already mentally switched roles and need to acknowledge that your brain is no longer in the game as it once was when dollars were involved.

It might seem like I am taking a rather low view of people's capacity to operate without funding, but the simple fact is that *money makes a difference*. Some who wish to head down this path may do so with the best of intentions, but soon discover they have lost focus and purpose. You can most definitely serve a church in an unpaid way, although it would be important to clarify the expectations of your role.

Reason 6: You Need More Money To Live

In the past, it was generally accepted that pastors would sacrifice financially and live on less than others because that was the nature of the role. Pastors couldn't appear wealthy, or to profit from the ministry, or it was said that they were being paid too much. While Paul chose to limit the support he received from churches to ensure that accusation would be groundless, there was also no doubting that he believed a worker was worthy of his/her hire.[2]

Even with the increased salaries pastors now earn, many still live their entire lives on a very modest income, and enter their later years with little to draw on. Some would say this is simply the cost of ministry, and it is the pastor's job to trust God for their financial future. It would be more accurate to say that it is for all of us to do this.

Just as Paul chose to reject any financial support, a pastor may also choose that course, however it is another thing entirely to have it imposed by others, to be kept poor by those who would not appreciate similar treatment in their own workplace.

While you can survive on a meagre amount of money if necessary, working outside the church should be seen as a valid option to bolster the family budget. Many professionals and tradespeople can easily earn two to three times the hourly rate of the pastor, meaning they can use the time outside the church to considerably boost finances.

Reason 7: You Don't Have To 'Come Out' Quite As Quickly

I have observed a variety of responses in people when I let them know I am a pastor. Some don't care, some are curious, and others definitely respond with a resistance and a distancing that has seen some potentially healthy new relationships fall flat before going anywhere.

I recall meeting my neighbour across the back fence shortly after moving into our new home. As we chatted, we discovered we were around the same age and stage of life, so I invited him and his wife around for a drink that same evening. There was a tangible warmth and receptivity for the first half of the night, until the conversation shifted to our jobs. I mentioned that I was a pastor as well as an irrigation repairer and then watched as the shutters snapped down and the guard went up. I don't know what experience he'd had with Christians before, but he wasn't up for another one. We never spoke again for more than a couple of minutes.

Responses aren't always as extreme as that, but nowadays I introduce myself as a small business owner and I have never experienced the same disengagement. Admittedly it's not exciting. It's a very garden variety sounding job, but neither does it have the potential for offence or instant 'social distancing'. In time, I let people know I am a Christian, involved significantly in a local church and subsequently that I am one of the pastors. By this point we are friends and the information is no longer delivered in a vacuum.

Reason 8: Your Prophetic Voice Is Not Tamed

Sometimes, as a pastor, certain things need to be said to a congregation, things that could well impact the giving or attendance in weeks to come. How many pastors have held back on speaking hard truths, or have trodden more cautiously than they would prefer because of the potential financial consequences? For example, to speak of greed in a church, where there is abundant wealth, may well be risky business. If, however, your livelihood is no longer solely dependent on those people, you can be less restrained. When you have a sustainable source of income outside of the church then you may be more likely to speak boldly to issues that require it.

Reason 9: You Understand How Other Non-Pastors Feel After A Hard Day

As a pastor it's been frustrating to show up to an evening Bible study group, only to hear that two people have stayed home because they had a 'hard day at work', or were just too weary after the commute to venture out again. I remember a leader in one church who would nod off at around 9.00 pm, just before the meeting was due to finish. As a full-timer, I had prepared for this meeting and wanted to make the best use of the time, and here he was nodding off.

I wanted to yell: "Wake up!"

In the last thirteen years I have felt his pain. Coming home from some brutally hard days in the summer sun, I have had to turn around and leave again thirty minutes later to lead a meeting. I couldn't even skulk in the background because I was facilitating, but everything in me just wanted to be in bed.

I think we sometimes forget how hard people work, and what they sacrifice to attend our meetings, so now if I notice someone looking weary, or taking a nap while I'm speaking, I just assume they have been working hard and probably need to catch-up on sleep. I understand their world much better.

Reason 10: Your Church Can't Afford A Full-timer

I have put this most common reason at the very end of my list, as this is certainly *not* the best reason to be bivocational, even though it was my own starting point when I was a youth pastor, employed two days per week to establish a youth ministry that was already stretching the church budget. If your church can't afford to employ you more than two or three days a week then you are inevitably going to rely on your spouse working, or finding additional work yourself to supplement your budget.

Many pastors find themselves in this situation, but it's often perceived as a problem that will be fixed once the church grows and the finances improve. Without a doubt, a change of mindset on your part will be the most important ingredient here: to see this as an opportunity rather than a roadblock. The church's finances may pick up but, if they don't, then it will be helpful to see the secular work as an opportunity to encounter life as the rest of the church community does.

AND 10 REASONS YOU MAY CHOOSE NOT TO BE BIVOCATIONAL

Maybe you're reading the ten reasons to consider being bivocational, and you're thinking: *but there are reasons you might not want to consider being bivocational and you haven't addressed them.*

I hear you. This approach to ministry may not suit everyone so, in the interests of fairness, let me list some of the downsides to being bivocational.

Reason 1: Your Identity Is Too Deeply Invested In Being A Full-Time Pastor

It may be that you cannot imagine being anything but a full-time pastor in a local church. Perhaps God has called you to this; if so then keep going.

But it's also possible that, for some people, their sense of identity is so deeply connected to their full-time pastoral role that not being in that position would unsettle them. It could even be that they see anything less than full-time ministry as a failure or a disappointment. This is leaning in the direction of seeing ministry as a superior calling, and other roles as lesser. The long-held perception of bivocational as the second-best option may be a result of this perspective. The full-time pastor is no more loved or valued for his/her ministry position than the full-time lawn mowing man. Sometimes simple pride in our position can prevent us from seeing other possibilities.

Reason 2: You Don't Do Multi-tasking Well

Not everyone can change gears easily from job to job. Some people really need to focus on one thing, and do it well, because the constant need to attend to two different roles leaves them exhausted and feeling like they are always behind. That said, we already multi-task when pastoring. We lead, teach, mentor, and so on. It may be that for those working in a completely different field (e.g. plumbing) it is the degree of difference in between plumbing and pastoring that results in feelings of disorientation or frustration.

Reason 3: Meeting With Other Staff Is Difficult

When there are four part-time staff, each working two days a week, the need to meet and stay on the same page is increased, however the chances of your work hours aligning in order to hold regular staff meetings is nigh on impossible. We have operated with a bivocational model for over twelve years now and, as our staff team has grown, so has the complication of finding a time to meet.

When we began working together it was with a dedicated hour of prayer from 7.00 am to 8.00 am each Friday, followed by a pastor's catch up. As people's work schedules changed, and others needed to drop children at school, we found these meetings impossible to maintain. As the team has grown we have found it difficult to replace this meeting because there isn't a point during the week when we are all free at the same time. Our current meeting at 4.00pm on a Friday is the best we could do, but it still means that, some weeks, someone is missing. It's a tension we simply have to live with. That said, if we aren't diligent about meeting with one another we could easily drift into working alongside but not together. There are no easy answers to this issue.

Reason 4: You Struggle To Manage Expectations

As well as your expectations of yourself, you have to contend with the expectations of other staff, your congregation, family, spouse, and maybe even your denomination. If you can't deal with the idea that you are not going to please everyone all the time – in fact, it is more than likely that you will occasionally disappoint people – then it's best you don't take on a bivocational gig.

If you are bivocational you will never be able to function at the capacity of a full-time pastor, nor should you expect this of yourself, but not everyone can manage this tension well.

If you are already bivocational, and struggling with this issue, then a good coach or supervisor will be invaluable in helping you along the way.

Reason 5: You May Find Yourself Constantly Busy

To be clear, this is largely a personal choice, but it can certainly feel busier running between two jobs than focusing on one. As already mentioned, if the expectation is that we will function much as a full-time pastor would, but in less time, then we will find ourselves busy beyond comprehension. Eventually, it will take a toll on our family life, and possibly our mental health.

It's not wrong to have intense periods of activity, but to be always busy is like driving a car constantly at 4000 rpm. There need to be times of idle and recovery, otherwise burnout or breakdown is inevitable. Not everyone can manage life in such a manner that they get the space, and rest, they desperately need. If you are not naturally self-disciplined, and able to create space for rest, then the bivocational life may be just the recipe for disaster.

Again, a good supervisor or coach will be able to help you reflect on why you need to be so busy, and offer strategies for living a simpler, slower-paced life.

Reason 6: Coordinating Holidays Is Difficult

Holidays are important. When we don't take them we risk becoming weary and over-worked. However, being employed by two organisations can make it more complicated to sync holidays. There may be specific constraints on when holidays can be taken (e.g. school teachers can only take school holidays). When combined with the challenge of working around other staff and their needs, it can become increasingly problematic. The larger a staff gets, the more complex it becomes to schedule holidays, but good administrative help can assist in better long-term planning. Whatever you do, don't neglect your annual leave! It's there for a reason.

Reason 7: It Is Difficult to Find Time To Attend Pastor's Networks

If you're going to be bivocational then you will simply have to accept that the regular networking meetings, conferences and gatherings, that other pastors attend, are not going to rank as highly on your priority list.

You have a smaller number of hours to complete a certain number of tasks, so it is hard to justify losing two of those hours to eat breakfast with other local pastors. I realise the value in these gatherings and, in the three years I was working full-time, I prioritised these events, recognising that if we are going to be effective in the community then we need to work collaboratively. However, joining events like these more recently has served as a reminder that I no longer belong in that world.

I distinctly remember arriving at a pastor's networking breakfast in a work shirt, shorts and boots because I was slotting the meeting in before heading off to install irrigation. I was one of the first to arrive, and sat down at the table only to have eyes look at me as if to say: "Who are you and what are you doing here?" A few laughs later and all was ok, but I realised I didn't fit in that space as others did.

Reason 8: You May Struggle With Success Envy

If you're bivocational, and in your mid-thirties, then you may well look around at those who are successfully climbing the ministry career ladder, being offered the plum jobs and becoming known and recognised around the country. Meanwhile, you're toiling away in a regular job at the same time as leading your church. Perhaps what you are doing seems insignificant, and you feel as though you need to prove your worth by getting one of those jobs. If you can't live with obscurity and invisibility then bivocational work will bring you undone.

As a bivocational pastor, you often fly under the radar, going largely unnoticed by peers and associates who have given themselves to ministry full-time. A commitment to faithful insignificance is a pre-requisite for a bivocational pastor. If the envy factor is too strong then you may not be suited to this type of work.

Solution? Go see a good counsellor and work through your success demons!

Reason 9: You May Not Have A Second Skillset That is Easily Used In Bivocational Ministry

It may be that the only jobs you have ever had are within the church. Your experience is only in Christian leadership, so you don't have marketable skills in other areas. You may need to consider either retraining, or starting at the bottom in an area you see as having potential. I realise that neither option is easy or attractive.

Alternatively, it may be that you are highly capable in various areas, but there is simply no way of finding part-time work in the roles for which you are qualified. If your previous work involved significant challenge and responsibility, then chances are it may not be possible to perform it part-time. My suggestion is that you can only ask your boss if it's feasible, and see what response you receive. You may be surprised.

Reason 10: You Just Don't Want To

Perhaps as you read and ponder you hear the value of bivocational mission and ministry, but you just don't feel up for the task of finding another job to work alongside your church employment.

You're worried that you might end up doing something you don't enjoy, earning less than you could as a full-time pastor, and generally feeling dissatisfied with life. You might be miserable *and* poor. You're right – that could happen – and it isn't ideal. I certainly wouldn't advocate placing yourself in a position where you know you will be frustrated daily and lacking in joy.

What should you do? I can only suggest prayer and listening to the Spirit to guide. If He calls you, then you go – whatever it looks like – because this is the nature of Christian discipleship. If He doesn't then maybe it just isn't for you. That's ok too.

––––––––

So while I wholeheartedly commend the bivocational life to pastors as the preferred mode for missional effectiveness, I appreciate that for some it is simply too difficult to manage. It may *not* be for you, perhaps because of your stage of life, your ability to juggle two separate roles, or because you just can't make the budget work. It may be that the profession you are qualified in has no opportunity for part-time work, and the only work you can find would be poorly paid and soul-destroying. You might be called to a full-time ministry position, or maybe you have been full-time in ministry for so long that it's hard to imagine anything else.

The bottom line is that it's of vital importance to know *why* you have embarked on your chosen pathway so that you can move forward with a considered plan, and an awareness of the limitations and temptations you will face.

FOR REFLECTION

- What has been your perception of people in bivocational mission and ministry over the years, and how has this perception shifted as you have experienced being bivocational?
- Which of the reasons *for* being bivocational do you identify with? Rank three of these in order of their prominence in *your* experience, with one being the most prominent reason.

- Which of the reasons *not* to be bivocational have been part of your experience, and how have you dealt with these?
- Do you have additional reasons 'for' or 'against' that have not been mentioned in this chapter?
- What would be an 'ideal' bivocational scenario for you and your family?

Notes

[1] That said, it is not automatically the case. It is possible to be 'in the world' and yet remain very separate and disconnected.
[2] (1 Timothy 5:18).

8

THE 'HOW' OF BECOMING BIVOCATIONAL

If you understand the reasons behind the pursuit of bivocational mission and ministry (the 'why?') then the obvious next step is to consider the 'how?' Most creative people like to understand 'why', and then create their own plan of action. Other more practical people just prefer to have a clear plan laid out for them. If you're in the latter group, then the next few chapters will provide a step-by-step process for moving yourself and your church community towards a bivocational way of ministry. If you prefer to chart your own course, the principles in these chapters will still be helpful. Reading them may even allow you to learn from my mistakes, rather than having to make the same ones yourself.

PRAY

It's obvious I know – so obvious that when I first drafted this chapter I left it out. That was partly because I assumed that, if you picked up a book on this subject, then you were already praying about this possibility, but let's be honest; this may not be the case. Sometimes we move in this direction because we're struggling financially, or we feel trapped in a role we are no longer passionate about, and we are just scratching around trying to find a solution.

So when I say 'pray', I mean more than just asking God if this is for you. That could be the end game but, in your prayer, listen for the 'desires of your heart', be conscious of the people God may be bringing into your life, of the way your circumstances may be curiously shaping up to make this a possibility. Be aware of how the Spirit is guiding your prayers in ways you haven't known previously. Be attuned to new stirrings and adventurous ideas, because these all may be the Spirit of God doing His work. In prayer you may also hear the Spirit say 'not for you' and that will save you and your family a world of unnecessary upheaval.

Of course, this kind of prayer takes time. It requires us to be still for longer periods and to hold a listening posture. If you are serious about making a change then be equally serious about creating space in your life, to hear the voice of God guiding and directing you.

Pray. Obvious, yes… but not always.

CONVERSATIONS YOU MUST HAVE

The bivocational life is possible for every pastor and every church but, if you intend to pursue this course and move away from operating as a full-time pastor, then before you take any practical steps, there needs to be a serious conversation with your church leadership to determine whether this is an arrangement they can genuinely support.

While some are forced into the bivocational sphere by declining church finances, unless the congregation can grasp that, with a decline in work hours comes a proportionate decrease in pastoral services, there will be tension. Many church cultures simply see the pastor as the person who must perform certain tasks, so dispensing these to congregation members may sound good in theory, but it does not always work in practice.

On the shifting of this understanding, Edington writes:

> *This means that in a bivocational model of ministry, something about the very nature of the community itself must undergo a shift from what is, in the Standard Model, typically a consumer or recipient ethos to a participant or stakeholder ethos.*[1]

If a bivocational approach to ministry is to work for both pastor and church, then it will succeed as *both* embrace and own their part in the agreement. The pastor will share typical pastoral tasks (teaching, care, leadership) with the congregation. In turn the church members, will take responsibility for these aspects of ministry as appropriate. Not every pastor can relinquish control while retaining a measure of authority and leadership. And not every congregation can step into performing tasks they have always assumed carry a level of gravitas that is beyond them. A careful conversation is needed to frame up how the bivocational approach works in practice.

Edington continues:

> *In either case, there's one overarching reality to grapple with upfront: the successful implementation of a bivocational model of ministry* **is a work of the entire faith community**, *and not just the ordained member (or members) of that community. 'Bivocational ministry' is much more than a shorthand description of the working*

life of the pastor of a church. It's a way of describing a different way of thinking about how the ministry of the whole community works.[2]

That last sentence is vital. In pursuing bivocational ministry, the *whole* church is being called to re-think who they are and how they operate – not just one man or woman.

There needs to an ongoing discussion about the changes that are occurring, and how both pastor and church are navigating them. Such a primal paradigm shift will need constant dialogue to ensure it is worked out well.

While there needs to be a conversation with the church and the leaders, the pastor also needs to have an equally important conversation with his or her spouse and family because the change will significantly impact marriage and family life. In a later chapter, we will explore the questions that need to be considered in order to minimise the number of nasty surprises, while ensuring some life-enriching outcomes for our loved ones. However, it needs to be said quite bluntly that, if your spouse is opposed to the idea of operating bivocationally, then it will be an uphill and potentially disastrous journey. Ensure there is at least agreement, but preferably enthusiastic consent before moving forwards.

WHERE TO PUT YOUR SPADE – EIGHT OPTIONS FOR FINDING WORK

If you intend to accept another paid role, the obvious starting point is with the trade or profession you were involved in before pastoring. This allows you to build on existing skills in an area where your capacities are strongest. Paul continued in the family business as a tentmaker, while the disciples saw fishing as their 'go to' if needed. Unless you transitioned straight from high school to Bible College (not recommended) then you will have an established or familiar way of making a living outside of being a pastor.

While that previous job may no longer have the same appeal, this is the first place to start when making ends meet. In the early years of ministry, I found myself relief teaching at my local school. As I got to know staff and students, I was offered a permanent part-time role. This was one of the most enjoyable times of my life, as I was able to work in a public school as a Christian teacher who was also known as a local youth pastor.

In writing about various bivocational employment options, Hugh Halter advocates for what he calls 'smart jobs':

> *'Smart jobs' are either a job that makes you a lot of money fast or a job that helps you connect with people and create social momentum. A super-smart job does both. A dumb job, therefore, would be one that does neither.*[3]

While it is ideal to think 'smart' and pursue this kind of role, it can sometimes be difficult locating part-time work in your field of expertise. My pastor friends whose previous jobs were in engineering tell me that it's virtually impossible to work part-time, or job share, because of the ongoing demands of the projects they are involved in. If the profession you are qualified for just won't suit the bivocational life at all, then it's time to explore other options.

1. Project/Contract Work. Many fields require people for specific contracts or projects, and when the work is complete there is no more obligation for either party, although good performance usually leads to further work. Picking up work of this sort allows you flexibility in working hours, while enabling you to continue working in a pastoral role.

It's helpful to consider whether you would prefer to work in a similar field to pastoring, such as coaching or consulting, or whether you would prefer to try something completely different. Whatever the case, don't be afraid to offer your services where you see a need. While we were planting a church in 2003, our denominational youth worker took a new path with his vocation, and there was no one providing oversight to the youth work or the pastors. I had some 'earning hours' left in my week so I proposed that I work twelve hours per week in a very specific coaching role, catching up one-to-one with youth pastors to help them reflect on the various aspects of their ministries. It was always going to be a short term 'fill in' role, but I still remember it as one of my most satisfying jobs and it began with an 'I wonder…' followed by a simple proposal.

2. Labouring. It isn't fancy, but there is always employment available for people prepared to work hard. The money is usually minimum wage, and the jobs are usually very physical, but many employers find it difficult to locate committed, reliable staff for these kinds of positions so, if you are willing to put in the effort, you may find yourself indispensable. The upside is that you won't need to visit the gym.

A friend in his fifties found himself separated from his wife, unemployed, and desperate for work just to survive. He eventually landed a physically demanding yard job with a steel fabricator. Within six months of being there he became highly regarded by the bosses for being a genuine, reliable worker, and was promoted accordingly. As an ex-pastor in a trade workshop, he found himself in the company of some hard-living young men with vastly different worldviews to his own. When he eventually left the job, his greatest regret was that he was leaving these relationships. Although the work itself was not particularly enjoyable, he chose to make it significant as he shared his life with his workmates, and had a positive influence on them.

So be sure to consider simple 'grunt work'. It will keep you fit, pay the bills, and place you amongst people whose worlds differ to your own. You will certainly hear and see things you wouldn't while cocooned in a pastoral office!

3. Start A Small Business. If you have a knack for new initiatives, and an entrepreneurial spirit, then you just might find energy in this space. Be warned though. Small business isn't for everyone as it requires diverse competencies and strong self-discipline but, if you have the energy, ideas and skills, then this is a great way to both earn income and, potentially, work in your local community.

How do you get started? Simply tap into a skill you have, or find a niche that isn't being filled, then fill it. A significant motivator in starting my own business was our disappointing experiences with many tradespeople who arrived late, didn't show, or whose workmanship and work ethic was poor. In the early days of running Brighton Reticulation, I was convinced that all I needed to do to gain work was: a) turn up on time; b) be polite, engaging and work hard; and c) charge a fair price and honour any warranties or guarantees. It was a perfect formula, and very soon the phone began to ring with new clients and word of mouth referrals.

During a summer holiday break, my daughter Ellie spent time painting various images on her clothing. The number of compliments she received led her to kick off a small venture in painting clothing for other people. Passion n Paint began as her hobby but, in time, it became her business. It's great to do something you love, but ultimately if it's a business venture it must also be sustainable and profitable. In 2022 Ellie graduated as a registered nurse, so her venture remains more of a hobby than a business project, however it is still something she can turn her hand to at any time if she wishes.

With a small business you have three significant components:

a) the service or product you are providing;
b) the marketing and advertising that generates the work; and
c) the management of scheduling, finances and invoicing.

Obviously, the more of these you manage yourself, the less you need to outsource and pay for; however it is rare to find someone with an aptitude in all three. But do not be fooled – having the skills for the job, whether that be irrigation, web design, painting, or something else, are not enough in themselves. If you can't generate work, or if you don't follow up on unpaid bills, then your business will slowly unravel before your eyes.

You can also buy a business, but there must be a significant amount of due diligence before making that kind of investment. Be especially wary of franchises, as these tend to be excellent money-spinners for the franchisor but often very poor return for the person working in the business. There is much more that could be said here about starting a business, but plenty of others have written about this in business start-up guides.

Once you have a business established you will, of course, develop a client base. You will form relationships with suppliers and with other operators. You will also face ethical challenges around how to cope with bad debt, deal with complaints, and manage finances with integrity. One of the recurring struggles in my own trade is the number of people who ask: "How much for cash?" They are obviously requesting a discount for not declaring the work to the tax office. Some people blatantly ask me if I can make the invoice out to the address of their rental property so they can claim it as a tax deduction. Everyone wants an honest tradesperson, but they aren't always prepared to keep their side of that deal. I know I have lost jobs because I won't do 'cashies', and I have found myself in some strong conversations with people who ask me for bogus invoices.

Running a business can be lucrative, profitable and energising if you can manage it well. Alternatively, you can find yourself constantly burdened with worry due to late payments, difficult clients or unforeseen expenses.

4. The Church Starts A Business

More and more churches are seeking to serve their communities as well as generate finance through small business ventures. Sometimes these funds can be used to support pastoral staff.

Quinns Baptist Church, where Danelle and I pastor, was invited to start an Out of School Hours Care facility that serviced the families who were part of both the local school and the church community. This venture was pursued by Danelle and one other woman, and together they managed to get it established, profitable and successful in just a couple of years. Danelle worked for several years in a management role, serving local families in a way that complemented her pastoral role.

Churches have opened cafes, art galleries and op shops, to name a few ventures. Perhaps your church can consider becoming involved in the neighbourhood by providing a much-needed service. You may be able to work in that business alongside the very people you are seeking to connect with. Win-win!

5. Retrain/Upskill/Study.

Perhaps you can find enough financial buffer in your budget to study for a qualification in an area that is currently inaccessible to you.

Over the years I have acquired a few skills in web design, coffee roasting, and drone photography, but not enough to back myself in business in any one of them. However, if I was able to complete courses that grew my capacities and my confidence, I would then be able to offer my services to a broader field. What is something you currently enjoy that could be income producing if you were to either upskill, or seek to do it more professionally?

Again, beware of engaging in any long and expensive study programs that may not contribute to the acquisition of a profitable skill. It's nice to pursue your dreams, but you also have to pay the bills, so you need to know that the end result will be genuine employment or a business opportunity.

And if you stumble across a brightly coloured website offering to help you make many thousands of dollars per week without leaving home, then click away fast! And if, as you leave the webpage, you are offered a discount on the course/product/scam then get out of there even faster. Don't be fooled by the 100% money-back guarantees and the glowing testimonials of apparently real people. Someone might be getting rich off that web page, but it won't be you.

Invest your time and money in learning that will genuinely upskill you for something you want to do, and chances are you will have an excellent opportunity of finding work in that field.

6. Low Demand Work. There are jobs where the bar to entry is very low. Nightfill work at a local supermarket pays reasonably well, and doesn't require any qualifications. Similarly, checkout attendants, café and retail work are possible avenues into the workforce.

The downside is that finding a job of this kind can be difficult and, when businesses have vacancies, they are often flooded with applicants. My suggestion is to give your resume to local shops and establishments you already frequent, and where you have rapport. Chances are you will then be considered seriously if there is a vacancy.

If you happen to land a job of this kind, then you have the opportunity to take it on in such a way that you bring the love of God into your workplace and turn routine, even tedious, tasks into something beautiful.

On a recent family holiday in the New South Wales town of Port Macquarie, we stumbled on Blue Cow Gelato, an ice cream shop where the young lady behind the counter offered such enthusiastic, genuine and friendly service that we left raving about her. Danelle and Sam went in first, but when they told me about her, I also ventured in for an ice cream myself, wondering if maybe she was just being nice to my good-looking son. Nope. There were two girls serving ice cream, and it was immediately evident which one she was. We even went back for more, just because she had done such an amazing job. No matter what you are doing, you can make an impact if you choose to do it with enthusiasm and passion.

7. Volunteer. If you want to work somewhere, but no positions are available, then one way to get noticed by the bosses is to offer your time for free, and then do the work to such a high standard that you cannot be ignored. Not every workplace can take volunteers but, if you can assist for even half a day each week, you may soon become a valued part of the team and they may want to keep you around. They might even create a position just for you.

In August 2018, I was chatting with a young guy in the surf who asked me if I had any jobs going. I had first met him in February of that year, and immediately sensed God telling me to pray for him. I prayed for him every day even though I hardly knew him and our paths rarely crossed. But here we were surfing, and he was seeking work. I told him I didn't have any need for him in winter. "But call me in October when I'm busy and I might need you." I appreciated his bold upfront approach, so I shouldn't have been surprised when, in early October, I had a call from him asking: "When do I start?"

I chuckled and told him I still didn't need anyone but, if he wanted to tag along for a couple of days, we could see whether he liked the look of the work and I liked the way he approached things. He immediately agreed. On the first morning, he was on my driveway, right on time and dressed for work. We attended several jobs that day and he sought to make himself useful to me whenever possible. He showed me his work ethic, and I was impressed. Two days later I still didn't need him, but I gave him a small payment for his time as he was helping me get home earlier. The next week I had hired him at an hourly rate, and he worked for me for nearly six months. In the final days, his work ethic and his assistance to me was in the 9/10 range. I enjoyed his company, and we had many valuable conversations around his vocational direction and the bigger questions of life. Don't diminish volunteering as wasted time. It just may be the door into an otherwise non-existent opportunity.

8. Consulting. Entering this area assumes you have a professional skill that is worth money. If you do, then why not use it to create income?

The huge upside to this type of work is the degree of flexibility and the high income. Typically, a consultant can make in a day what a pastor would make in a week. You largely determine your own working hours, and set your own hourly rate. You can choose to set it low and attract a lot of work, or you can set it higher and only take on the work you need.

If you want to be bivocational, and have capacity in this area, consulting could be worth exploring. The challenge will be carving out a niche for yourself, so it may not be a quick start role but, if you can survive the start-up phase and generate some work, chances are that you will be able to earn an excellent income, engage with people and have time in reserve for other mission and ministry work.

WHAT'S STOPPING YOU?

Which of the above options could work for you in this season of life?

The next challenge is to make something happen – to set a process in motion and move towards the outcome you are hoping for. It may be that you dip your toe in the 'bivocational water' by just working one day in another field while holding onto your full-time pastoral role. It may be that you put more time and effort into a hobby that has genuine business potential to see if it might fly.

If you see the missional potential, and want to move in this direction, then it will begin with some concrete action on your part. Nothing will change until you take the initiative and intentionally pursue a course of action.

FOR REFLECTION

1. What ideas or feelings stir in you as you read this chapter?
2. Can you imagine yourself in another vocational activity? If so, what do you see?
3. Who do you need to discuss these ideas with, and in what order should you approach these people?
4. What obstacles should you expect to encounter along the way, and how will you deal with them?
5. What would need to change in the way you currently pursue ministry for this to be a sustainable future path?
6. If all goes well, what would you hope for as a 'best outcome'?
7. What risks may you need to take to transition into bivocational mode?

Notes

1. Edington, Mark D. W., *Bivocational*. (Kindle Locations 202-204). Church Publishing Inc. Kindle Edition. Location 199 of 1956
2. Edington, Mark D. W., *Bivocational*. (Kindle Locations 202-204). Church Publishing Inc. Kindle Edition. Location 199 of 1956
3. Halter, Hugh, *BiVO: A Modern-Day Guide for Bi-Vocational Saints*. Missio Publishing. Kindle Edition.

9

FIRST THINGS FIRST

The great challenge when bivocational is to lead a church *well*. That is all the more difficult if you intend to lead like pastors who are full-time, and follow the 'Western script', of a Sunday centred, often busy, programmatic church. Expecting to work at the same pace as them isn't realistic, and will likely see you burn out quickly. The first thing to do as a bivocational pastor is to set goals and expectations that are fair and reasonable, and also shared by the rest of your leaders.

The key here is to meet with your leaders and, *together*, set your understanding of success. This should align with both scripture, and your calling and capacity, rather than trying to fit in with the expectations of evangelical pop culture or with what everyone else is doing.

This is a critical stage in the process because, if the priorities set at this juncture are unclear, then the plans and processes that follow will not work as intended.

Where do we start? Let me offer three foundational ideas that need to be considered if we are to navigate this territory well. To some degree, these are obvious, even non-negotiable, but I include this chapter because, when time is tight, it can be easy to veer into pragmatism and fail to pay attention to the more critical components of healthy Christian leadership.

DEFINE SPIRITUAL LEADERSHIP

If the core task of the pastor is to lead a community of people, then central to that task is knowing what healthy spiritual leadership looks like, and the direction in which you are leading them. What exactly is it that is required from a pastor, and what is less important?

If you attend leadership conferences, and read the myriad of books on church leadership, then you might be convinced that 'Christian flavoured' management training is essential. You need to be competent at vision, strategy and change management. Unfortunately, it's possible to develop competency in these areas and see this as core business, when in reality they are peripheral to what we are actually called to do. Drawing on the journals of Eugene Petersen, Winn Collier writes of Petersen's bewilderment at the type of pastoral leadership he discovered he was being shaped for:

> *The ink on my ordination papers wasn't even dry before I was being told by experts, so-called, in the field of church that my main task was to run a church after the manner of my brother and sister Christians who run service stations, grocery stores, corporations, banks, hospitals, and financial services.*[1]

Petersen's prophetic voice, calling us to a life centred on Jesus, has been a breath of fresh air in a church world dominated by professionalism and KPIs.

No matter where you look in the New Testament, being adept at vision and strategic planning is not the central goal of spiritual leadership. Rather, it is about forming a community of people into Christlikeness. *This* must be at the core of any pastoral leadership, and takes priority over generating numerical growth, initiating building projects, or creative missional ventures. A pastor must take on the mantle of seeing that formation occurs, and that people are empowered to serve and flourish in both their character and their gifts.

It was CS Lewis who said:

> *The Church exists for nothing else but to draw people into Christ, to make them little Christs. If they are not doing that, all the cathedrals, clergy, missions, sermons, even the Bible itself, are simply a waste of time. God became Man for no other purpose.*

The source of Lewis's thinking was most likely the apostle Paul who, among others, had much to say on this subject. Paul offers several descriptions of what he considered to be his core task:

- In Colossians 1:28–29, he wrote that he hoped to 'present everyone fully mature in Christ'.
- In Galatians 4:17-20, he writes of this again saying: "I am in the pains of childbirth until Christ is formed in you".

- Then in 2 Corinthians 3:17-18, Paul writes of Christians everywhere 'being transformed into His (Jesus) image with ever increasing glory'.
- And in Romans 8:29 he speaks of our eternal destiny as being 'conformed to the image of God's Son'.

If this is the goal, and the pastor is leading the people in pursuing this outcome, then priority will be given to the activities that achieve this end. In their excellent book, *Renovation of the Church*, Kent Carlson and Mike Lueken argue that we should all be able to answer one simple question: *How do people become like Jesus around here?* It assumes one specific goal, and then asks for the means by which to accomplish that goal. As Carlson and Lueken intentionally sought to transition a church built on consumer principles, to one based on discipleship principles, they realised:

> *We started teaching on the necessity of Christ being formed in our people, and we realized that some in our congregation never signed up for that. We discovered that people weren't necessarily coming to church to be formed in the image of Christ.*[2]

HOW DO PEOPLE BECOME LIKE JESUS AROUND HERE?

Spiritual leadership begins with knowing that the goal is forming people into the likeness of Christ. Good spiritual leadership is the kind that has a plan for doing this effectively. While this priority ought to be the same for both full-time and bivocational pastors, the challenge of being bivocational is to harness and focus the limited time available to maximise your influence in this direction. The great temptation will always be to give your time to the things that are either urgent, measurable, or highly visible, functioning as a project manager, or CEO, however the business of forming people into Christ is often unseen, difficult to measure and occurs over long periods.

In our own community, where I only have two paid days of pastoral work, I have tried to promote a simple strategy to follow if we are to grow into Christlikeness. The plan is this:

1) Train yourself to be godly. Paul advises Timothy that physical exercise has some benefits, but spiritual discipline has benefits both now and in eternity, so it should be a higher priority (1 Tim 4:7).

If people genuinely want to become like Jesus then they will make moves to 'train themselves'. I unashamedly call people to take this first step and not to blame the church for any spiritual flabbiness. I remind people: "Your Christlikeness is your responsibility". No one can drag or force you into becoming like Christ, so it starts with you. Without a genuine inner life and connection to God, I have limited capacity to help others come close to Him, so giving time to nurturing my faith is a top priority.

As a pastor I try to meet with people who want to grow in Christlikeness, but I do not chase those for whom this is not a priority. I don't have time for trying to make people do things they just don't want to do. To this end, we try to teach people different methods of engaging with God, such as silence, journaling, and meditation. What we *can't* do is the actual work of creating space to be with God. We simply have to trust that, if people are sufficiently motivated, then they will do this work themselves and the benefits will show.

2) Help one another become Christlike. While I completely believe that your Christlikeness is your responsibility, I also completely believe that your Christlikeness is *my* responsibility, and my Christlikeness is *your* responsibility. In other words, we are in this together. We will live in community in such a way that we encourage, correct, rebuke and love one another into the likeness of Jesus.

There is no solitary discipleship. We need authentic interactions with other people to form us into Christ's image. It requires us to proactively create space to be with one another in a way that we talk openly about our lives and relationships with God. To that end, I encourage people to find an hour or so in their week to meet with one or two others to read scripture, check-in with each other, confess sin, and pray for one another. This is not complicated stuff.

As a church with many young families and workers making long commutes, we have found it difficult to establish the typical family home groups. One parent may come while the other stays home, but it often feels somewhat of a difficult experience as groups form very slowly, and people are absent. The idea of just two or three people meeting is manageable, though, and that is the key to establishing these processes. Alongside this are mens' and womens' groups which function with a high level of vulnerability and transparency, enabling people to share their lives with one another and be honest about their struggles.

The pastor's job here is to keep this priority before the people, calling them to step up and enter into these kinds of relationships. A bivocational pastor, whose focus is on formation, will quickly recognise that a very simple process is needed that doesn't rely on his or her involvement, but is owned and driven by those in the church.

3) Real life = real learning. It's great to spend time in scripture and prayer, both alone and with one another, but the rub is really how it all works out in everyday life. We try to do the daily activities of life with those we are in community with. We eat together, surf together, holiday together and, as we do, there are opportunities for learning and growth.

A little while back we headed off camping with another family from church. After spending time in Karajini National Park in the north of Western Australia, we then ventured into the old ghost town of Wittenoom. There are only two or three people who still live, completely off-grid, in this remote ex-asbestos mining town.

On the day we arrived in Wittenoom, we took a short drive around what's left of the town, a ramshackle collection of old buildings. As we did so, we noticed that the gem shop – the only functioning shop left in town when we last visited – had burnt down. We stopped the cars to take a closer look. Once inside the building, the kids discovered hundreds of gemstones. The place had burnt to the ground, yet no one had claimed these beautiful, polished rocks of all varieties. Our children began to fill their pockets.

They thought they had struck gold.

As we drove out to camp that day, everyone was ecstatic about their haul of goodies. The stones were washed and analysed and sorted. That evening by the campfire, the other father raised a question. "I'm not sure we should have taken those stones," he said. "I wonder if we did the wrong thing." I had felt similar, but was waiting for the right moment to raise it. Bernie just jumped right in.

And so began a valuable conversation. As we sat around the campfire, our families grappled with the question of right and wrong. It was one of the most practical classes in theological ethics I have participated in, as parents and children debated the merits of different positions. Regardless of age, everyone was offered the chance to make a case for what we should do.[3]

This is how discipleship happens – in the flow of life – as we encounter real issues, measure them against scripture, alongside the person of Jesus, and then respond with action. I have the sense that all present around that campfire outside Wittenoom learnt more in that one experience than in all the sermons they heard that year.

If you are bivocational and wondering how to find the time to effectively disciple people, my advice is to ensure you are in relationship with those in your community, and then simply make the most of the everyday opportunities that come along. I have discovered that much of my best discipleship has taken place with the young men who have worked for me over a summer. They see me day in, day out in favourable and unfavourable situations, and they observe what the life of faith looks like. Inevitably, this provokes conversation, and discipleship takes place on the job and in the moment.

Many 'real life' scenarios can be used intentionally if it is part of our focus. In this way, a bivocational pastor can be engaged in spiritual formation while repairing a car, surfing, fishing or even watching sport. Any time we do one of these everyday activities with others, we can influence them towards Christlikeness as we live in ways that reflect Jesus.

MINISTERING FROM A CENTRED LIFE

Several years ago I had a wonderful and transformative conversion experience when one of my friends – a Catholic turned atheist – managed to sneak under my guard. Before meeting Mike, I unashamedly drank instant coffee, sometimes eight a day, and while I knew that International Roast was pure evil, and Moccona Gold was the 'good stuff', I discovered that I didn't know coffee at all. In my defense this was the early 2000s when *no one* knew coffee.

"Let me make you a *real* coffee," Mike said as I entered his home for the first time. He explained the way he ground the beans right before using them so they didn't go stale, how to get a perfect pour through the portafilter, and the correct way to texture velvety, smooth milk. For him, this was a labour of love, and the result was beyond anything I had ever imagined possible. If this was coffee then what had I been drinking?

I was soon hanging out at Mike's house regularly, sipping lattes and learning how to roast green beans in a breadmaker with a heat gun. I bought my own Espresso machine and set up my own roasting equipment so I could always have fresh beans. That was nineteen years ago and I have not had an instant coffee since.

Nothing moves people like a person with real passion and dedication to their cause.

I am convinced that the reason we do not see more people coming to know Jesus isn't because we lack the capacity to articulate the Christian message, or the strategic competency to cultivate spaces where the gospel can be shared. Rather, the problem is that when we are called on to share the hope we have in Jesus, the story just doesn't have the punch we'd like it to have. We may even feel like we are mouthing a spiel we learnt somewhere and haven't used for years, and we struggle to own the words we hear ourselves speak. I know because, sadly, that has been my own experience at times.

But it was Jesus himself who said: "Out of the overflow of the heart the mouth speaks".[4] We can't help but speak about our passions and, when we know Jesus in a real way – because we have been with Him – we will not be able to contain the good news He offers. No theology degree is necessary, no evangelistic training required – just a heart aligned to His and a personal experience to share. In Acts 4, Peter and John are called to account for their healing of the lame man. Luke writes:

> *When they saw the courage of Peter and John and realised that they were unschooled, ordinary men, they were astonished and they took note that these men had been with Jesus.*

Unschooled, ordinary men and women, who had been with Jesus, were quite literally changing the world. Nothing matters more to the bivocational leader than ensuring there is 'fuel in the tank' – a fresh and ongoing relationship with the one we claim to follow. How you do that is completely up to you. No one can do the work of the spiritual disciplines for you, nor should anyone prescribe how you should be making your connections with God.

What is certain is that for your leadership to have credibility, and to form people into Christ, it has to come from lived experience deep in the gut, rather than clever theories of the head. It must echo a genuine encounter with Jesus. If it doesn't, your people will know, and it just won't fly. Any competent leader can run a church, organise meetings, and develop strategies, but what is most needed from a pastor is the ongoing experience of knowing and following Jesus, as well as the ability to help others have these transformative encounters.

As a bivocational pastor, it will always be tempting to skip the disciplines and practices that form us, and to get on with the various tasks that demand your time. But a pastor who isn't ministering from a centred life is worse than no pastor at all.

There are countless books that can help you engage in practices that form you and allow you to encounter Jesus, but the bottom line is that it must happen and it has to be real. You cannot rely on your organisational skills, or preaching skills, to get you by. Your energy must come from a life earthed in a relationship with Jesus.

I remember setting off to church-plant in 2003 and as part of the process I asked various people for their best piece of mission advice. *What would you do if you were in my shoes?* One of the people I asked was mother-in-law, Val, who is a fairly natural evangelist. When I asked, she pondered for just a moment and then said, "I would just live my ordinary life." At the time I was disappointed that this was all she had to offer. I wanted something innovative, insightful and inspirational and she gave me an answer that felt somewhat bland. However in time the truth of what she said began to dawn on me. An ordinary life centred on Jesus, surrendered and attentive to him is always going to be a catalyst for authentic mission.

SET AN APPROPRIATE CULTURE FOR BIVOCATIONAL CHURCH LIFE

If you are the pastoral team leader, and you are taking care of your own spiritual formation, then the next priority will be to work with your team and establish the culture and tone for how the church will function as a discipling entity.

When we first joined Quinns church in 2009, I discovered we didn't have a website, so I set my hand to that task. I knew I needed some content for the 'about us' page – the section that gives people a sense of who you *really* are. Having seen too many disconnects between glamorous web descriptions and actual church experience I attempted to describe accurately the people we are:

> *If you're looking for glitz, pizzazz, shiny happy people with perfect teeth and kids who never muck up then you might have to go somewhere else... However, if you're looking to be part of a pretty earthy bunch of people who are just doing their best at loving God, loving one*

> *another and loving the community around them then you'll probably slot right in.*

My co-pastor, Ryan, later encapsulated it in just two words: 'shoes optional'. I have lost count of the people who came to visit and then stayed, firstly because that sounded like the kind of church they wanted to be a part of, and secondly because we actually *were* those people.

If I wasn't bivocational, then we would still be these people; however, the choice to keep things simple, down-to-earth, and relationally driven, means that our bivocational team is rarely stretched to breaking point just to make the Sunday event happen. It's not impossible to pull off a high tech, extravagant Sunday event while working bivocationally, but it would mean significant time spent coordinating the people involved as your own capacity for participation will be limited.

While we have no desire to be sloppy and disorganised, our culture is intentionally relaxed, simple and relational. For many years we survived with only a handful of musicians. As a result, for a period of time, we made one service every month a non-musical event around tables. It was a little clunky and awkward, but our culture of simplicity meant we weren't going to risk burning people out for the sake of including music.

It will be helpful to describe the kind of culture you hope your church will have, and then set to moving it in that specific direction with some regular communal practices. If you intend to lead your people in a particular direction, you have to know who you aspire to be. If this isn't clear then *they* will lead *you* back to what is familiar, safe and comfortable for them – even if it doesn't work for you (or them).

Communal practices are simply the things we do together that express or affirm our identity. In our current church, for example:

- We don't have rosters for set up, pack up, and morning tea. We operate as a family and trust that people will contribute as they are able. Some Sunday's morning tea is sparse, but the following week is always a winner. That's just how it is.
- Our men's group eats together monthly with no agenda. The conversation ranges from the trivial to the deeply significant, but there is no script to work from or questions to answer. The value is genuineness in relationships. We believe that as we eat and as we share life, any need will be tabled in a trusted community. It works, and the absence of any pressure to reveal yourself allows people to tread into this water slowly if they wish to.
- A friend speaking to me about the culture of our church once said: "At Quinns, there's no shallow end". That's both a compliment and a problem. We do tend to 'get real' quickly in our conversations, but this feels threatening for some people. We have chosen this culture, for better or worse; it doesn't suit everyone.
- When people visit our church no one tries to convince them to stay. Our standard invitation to a newcomer is: "See how it feels around here and, if we feel like your people, then please stay; we'd love to have you. But if our culture doesn't feel like 'home' to you, then we can help you find a local church that is more in line with how you worship." It takes the pressure off both the church and the newcomer, and allows them to explore freely and leave easily if they need to.
- We allow children to 'free range' at church. Sometimes this means small children wander across the platform during worship. We let them go unless they are causing a scene and being overly distracting. In this, we are saying together that we want our children to be in the gathering and worshiping with us. We

realise that different parents will approach this situation in a variety of ways. We are ok with this and, if you join us, then you will need to be ok too.
- We have people who are King James reading fundamentalists, and those who are a good way up the progressive end of the theological spectrum. We agree on the essentials, if not the peripherals. We agree not to fight over non-essential theology. Those who try to start these fights find that either no one wants to fight them, or a leader will meet with them and encourage them to 'let it go'.
- We operate with a bare-bones approach to programmed activity because we don't want to be responsible for making people unnecessarily busy. We let activities die rather than staff them with people who don't want to be there.
- We don't challenge people to tithe. We encourage them to be exceedingly generous, and to share their money with whomever God directs them to. We do ask that if you are part of the family, and you 'eat from the fridge', that you share in the household budget as you can.
- We also say that 'if you are in the family then you do the dishes', as a way of indicating that we all have jobs to do – some are visible and some are behind the scenes. But if this is your family then we expect you to serve the family in some way.

None of these cultural elements are written down anywhere, but over time we have come to recognise the way we do things and what matters to us. This is true of every community even if we aren't always conscious of it.

These are the bigger picture priorities that need attention and focus before moving on to the details of how bivocational ministry happens in a local church, and some of the more challenging specific issues that a bivocational pastor will face. Some have suggested that the time constraints on bivocational pastors make ministry more difficult than it would be otherwise, but I choose to believe that the time constraints actually serve to make us more focused and purposeful.

FOR REFLECTION

- What does success look like for you? Describe specific markers that would show you had achieved what you set out to do.
- "How do people become like Jesus around here?" How would you answer that question for your own church?
- The way a 'centred life' looks will depend on your current life stage. How does it look for you at present?
- If you aren't living a life centred on Jesus, then what can you change to put this key element in place?
- Describe the culture of the church you hope for. If this is different from the church culture you currently experience, how can you help the church change directions?
- What visible practices/behaviours would you want to see as expressions of your culture? For example, if informality is an important part of the culture, then the freedom to dress as you wish would be a priority.
- Which part of this chapter did you find most challenging personally and what action may you need to take?

Notes

[1] Petersen

[2] Kent Carlson; Mike Lueken, *Renovation of the Church: What Happens When a Seeker Church Discovers Spiritual Formation.* (Kindle Locations 1267-1268). Kindle Edition.

[3] It was decided by consensus that the most Christlike response would be to visit the lady, explain the situation and see if she wanted the stones returned. In the end, she appreciated the visit, but let the kids keep the stones.

[4] Luke 6:45

10

THE NUTS AND BOLTS OF A SUSTAINABLE BIVOCATIONAL MINISTRY

The previous chapter focused on the non-negotiable, essential components of a healthy and sustainable ministry. But what do you do once you've got your ship afloat and pointing in the right direction? How do you manage your time to make the most valuable contribution to your church? If you only have two or three days available, you can't afford to waste those hours on non-essential or low-priority activities. Some of us are naturally task-oriented people, and we come alive in the completion of specific jobs, while others are people-oriented and thrive on human interaction. It's helpful to know which way you are wired, but it is also important to know that however you are wired, you need to be able to function competently across both areas.

The key challenges that bivocational pastors face in making things work fall into two primary areas:

a) **Teams** – how we manage the people side of mission and ministry. In a bivocational role you will lead some projects on your own, but being part of healthy teams where responsibility can be delegated will be critical to your effectiveness.
b) **Tasks** –There are many tasks you can put your hand to in ministry, but knowing where to best invest your time is essential.

TEAMS

If you are going to have both longevity and effectiveness in any ministry, then you must think 'team'. Jesus recruited twelve to be with Him and to learn from Him. There was no sense that He was a lone ranger. If He relied on others to help Him then so will you, and the need for teams is amplified in the bivocational setting where your time is constrained.

The ability to recruit and empower teams to serve will be the difference between surviving and flourishing, so it's vital to acknowledge this reality and build the competencies of others around you.

BUILD A (5Q) TEAM

As an ex-basketballer, I remember the importance of having all five key roles on the court filled by people who could actually do their jobs well. It was great to have a smart point guard to run the plays, but a complete team needed a tall, dominant centre, an athletic power forward, a sharp shooting guard, and a versatile swingman to perform optimally. Lose competency in any one of those roles and the team would suffer. Alternatively, field a team of five-point guards and you are on a road to disaster! Teams need leaders, but they also need to be balanced.

Similarly, if you're going to be bivocational then I suggest you identify quickly where you fit in the APEST framework, and then build a team with those whose gifts and orientations complement your own.[1] Using Ephesians 4:11-16, Alan Hirsch identifies the core DNA of every church as being composed of apostles, prophets, evangelists, shepherds and teachers. Hirsch argues these people are present in the DNA of *every* church and, if we will take the time to find them and empower them for service, then the church will be richer for the experience. Whether or not you agree with Hirsch, that every church has these gifts present as part of their DNA, you cannot deny that every church would be enriched and balanced by their presence and activity.

In defining these gifts Hirsch uses the following descriptors:[2]

> **Apostle – the pioneer.** From the Greek word 'apostello', meaning the sent one. Apostles see new opportunities and pursue new initiatives. They give genuine missional impetus to the team.

> **Prophet – the truth teller.** Prophets will both question the status quo, and call us back when we deviate from the path God has called us to.

> **Evangelist – the recruiter.** Evangelists naturally draw other people into the mission. As a result, much of their focus is outside the church community.

> **Shepherd – the nurturer.** Shepherds protect and care for the people. They focus on forming people into spiritual maturity.

Teacher – the communicator. Teachers are able to explain Biblical truth in ways that common people can grasp.[3]

We may each have one or more of these gifts, but it is typical for Western churches to be lacking apostles, prophets and evangelists because we have been living with a Christendom mindset for so long. We have only needed shepherds and teachers to maintain the status quo, so our pioneers, entrepreneurs and provocateurs have often sought to use their God-given gifts either in the marketplace, or with para-church groups.

The simple exercise of discerning the gifts of our team members will not only allow them to function at their best, but also help the team know who to turn to when challenges arise. When considering adventurous moves as a church (my natural apostolic instinct) I need to hear from those with a pastoral gifting as to how it will impact various people, and from the prophetic types who may have some left-field kind of insight to share.

If anyone had the capacity to go it alone in ministry, then surely it was Jesus. He is the '5Q man', embodying apostle, prophet, evangelist, pastor and teacher. Right from the start, though, He focused on recruiting and building a solid team of co-workers who would share the load with Him. These people observed and learned from Him as He engaged in various forms of ministry. They practiced various tasks in His presence (healing, casting out demons) and, as He trained them, He also devolved more of the work to them.

Jesus chose twelve to be with him, to learn from him and then to put into practice the things they had been taught. This was His method and it was very effective.[4] The great challenge in bivocational ministry is that team building takes time, and lots of it. Your team meetings may be formal gatherings, where one person runs through a businesslike agenda, or a more informal, conversational gathering. Either way, they must happen, and responsibility must be shared rather than carried by one person.

Not only is this team work a pre-requisite for being bivocational, it is actually one of the privileges of working in this way. Your church will *not* be driven by one star player, but by a team of people who realise their need for one another.

HOW TO RECRUIT A HEALTHY TEAM

A vital part of forming a good team is knowing *how* to ask people to join you. Jesus called Peter and John to be 'fishers of men':

a) **He spoke *their* language** and He helped them imagine the task in front of them.
b) **He invited them into a challenging space.** If a service opportunity is presented as a low demand, low importance role, and you are asked to simply 'turn up if you can', you will *not* recruit high capacity people. For the most part, high-quality people would rather invest time in meaningful activity – even if it is costly and sacrificial – than give occasional effort to an activity that was deemed unimportant. Don't be afraid to make the big ask!
c) **He gave them clear instructions for what to do and He trained them to do it**. Jesus called His disciples to preach the kingdom of God, heal the sick and cast out demons. His request was massive, clear and inspiring. He then taught and demonstrated the 'how', before sending them out.

A clear call to share in a valuable project, and to commit to specific action, will more often evoke the best from people, or at very least it will sort the committed from the interested. An ambiguous or vague request to 'come and do some ministry' will be unlikely to inspire; it may even confuse. Don't be timid and vague when calling a team together. Be bold.

Building a team is not negotiable. It must happen, but the choice will be between building a team of co-leaders, gifted differently, but who own the ministry just as much as you, or building a tribe of minions who lend a hand when asked, but have little ownership and passion. Secure leaders, who understand the importance of developing others, will seek out quality people and then ask them to give their best.

TRAINING YOUR TEAMS

It's unfair to enlist people in ministry roles (formal or informal) without at least some rudimentary orientation and training. When I think of training I look to Jesus' methodology which was so simple and yet so effective. He chose people in whom He saw potential, and then taught them in various settings, engaged in ministry with them and then sent them out in pairs to do it without Him.

From my days in youth ministry, I remember a simple process that helped me ponder what training may look like for those around me. It depicts Jesus' approach quite accurately:

> I do it – they watch
> I do it – they help
> They do it – I help/reflect with them
> They do it, and I do something else

There is no prescribed length of time for each of these stages, simply an awareness that different tasks require different training experiences, and that people need to be shown the task, supported as they attempt it, enabled to reflect on their experience, and then entrusted with responsibility to make it happen.

While there is some value in a classroom setting, the most effective ministry training always happens in the moment as we are confronted with a challenge. When we speak of training teams, our default mental picture is often of a room full of people passively listening to an instructor talk, but the kind of training people respond to best is the kind that involves them in the process. Think apprenticeships rather than classrooms.

Jesus taught His disciples and let them observe His work. Then He sent them out in pairs to heal the sick, cast out demons, and preach the kingdom of God. When they returned He helped them reflect on their experience. Sometimes they reported success, and other times they had questions about what went wrong. The point is that He actually trained them, and then trusted them to act upon what He had taught them. Those ministry tasks are the focus of the next section.

TASKS

Whatever your role, some tasks need to be completed, either by you or by others. This is largely why you have been employed. What matters is being *clear* on what the core tasks are. The nature of ministry means that we can easily slide into areas where we are most at ease, but not where we are most needed. Using your limited time effectively to do things that matter is always going to be a challenge.

DO WHAT ONLY YOU CAN DO

A recurring theme in the pastors I surveyed is that we should give our best energy to the areas in which we are most gifted. The great strength of the bivocational approach is that you are not expected to be all things to all people, so you shouldn't make a rod for your own back by trying. Instead, focus your energy on what you have been called to, and what you have been uniquely gifted for.

Paul saw himself as the apostle to the Gentiles, a missionary, and a church planter. As a result, he spent his time in evangelism and teaching new converts. We don't hear of him helping out at the Antioch soup kitchen on a Tuesday night, or writing the risk assessment for the men's fishing getaways. He was an apostle and teacher, and he spent his time on activities related to these giftings.

Likewise, it's important to be clear on your own gifts and calling to ensure your time is used effectively, and the church benefits. You may feel constrained by this, but I would encourage you to see it as an opportunity to excel at what you do best. My wife, Danelle, and I co-pastor but there are times when I defer to her expertise and vice versa. If we happen to be in a sensitive pastoral care situation together, then I will let her lead the way as she is more gifted in this area than I am. However, when it comes to teaching the Bible, or bigger picture leadership, she will sit back and allow me to take more of those roles. In a traditional model of church I would be a sole pastor, and required to be the primary pastoral carer for the whole church. While I can certainly serve in this way, it means I spend less time in my strengths, and the congregation does not receive the best pastoral care, or the best of my leadership capacity.

The only caveat I would add here is that sometimes you just have to do things you neither enjoy nor are good at, and 'it's not my gift' cannot be used as an excuse.

THE TWO ESSENTIALS OF LEADING A CHURCH

If your bivocational role involves serving as a sole pastor or a team leader, then two areas of priority must be leadership and communication. These aren't optional. You will be called on to give the mission and ministry shape and focus, and you will need good communication skills to enable this to happen. If you are apostolic in gifting, then your leadership and communication will reflect this. Similarly, if you are pastoral or prophetic, your primary gifting will shape your approach to leadership and communication. But you *must* undertake these two core tasks well to fulfil your role and enable the church to flourish.

A capable leader is committed to the core task of making disciples, and is able to gather capable people around them to ensure this happens. The leader also needs to be the one with their head up looking to the future, and discerning what the Spirit may be saying regarding the church. A good leader will spend a significant amount of time on tasks that are *not* pressing, but that will end up contributing to the health of the community.

In the Eisenhower Decision Making Matrix, as summarised in the table below, this is known as the 'non-urgent – important quadrant'.[5] It's too easy for a part-time staff member to get caught up reacting and responding to immediate crises and challenges, or dealing with this week's rosters and emails. These non-urgent activities take time away from the higher priority tasks that a team leader needs to be attending to.

Urgent/Important	**Urgent Non/Important**
Crises	Some phone calls
Emergencies	Some meetings
This week's sermon	Some emails
Pressing problems	Text messages

Non urgent/Non-Important	Non-Urgent/Important
Organising your desk Archiving emails Meetings with non-key people	Forward planning Relational development Values clarification Strategic teaching prep

The vitality of the church depends largely on leadership looking ahead to what will be required in two, five or ten years' time. If you are a co-pastor rather than team leader you will not carry this leadership mantle as heavily, but you will still need to think 'non-urgent/important' as a priority.

The other essential quality for almost every pastor is the ability to communicate sensitively and competently with the church community. I have used the term 'communication' broadly as some of this will certainly involve teaching the Bible, some will be helping a leadership team understand strategies for ministry, while some will be one-to-one conversations, or possibly communicating via email.

Leadership happens primarily by example, but also largely through communication. Unless you have a non-traditional form of church, your community will be looking to you as their primary source of teaching. We can argue about the place of the sermon in the church, and how effective learning occurs, but the simple reality is that whoever teaches and communicates well will have the ear of the people.

After these two priorities of leadership and communication are attended to, I suggest you play to your strengths with the hours that remain, and do the things God has created you to do. It may be that you are an excellent administrator who can organise the church well. Perhaps you are genuinely pastoral, so you are regularly seeking out the hurt, broken and needy to help guide them to Jesus.

In speaking to our church, I happily tell them that I lead, teach and meet with men. Those are my three core tasks and, if I focus on these, chances are I will be on track with what I am hoping to accomplish. It's not that I don't, or won't, meet with women (I do) but rather that I have a sense of calling to meet with men for frank conversations around life and faith. I must also do a small amount of administration, but it's minimal and I choose not to give more time to it than necessary. So being a part-timer allows me to focus on my strengths, and work from my gifts rather than being tied to fulfilling a particular pastoral paradigm.

In order to function effectively as a pastoral leader, you simply cannot allow yourself to be ruined by unrealistic expectations and demands. If you don't set a boundary around your own identity and contributions, then you will find yourself called on for anything and everything that your congregation considers to be the role of the pastor.

Do the things that *only* you can do, and recruit others for the tasks you are less competent at or gifted for. And don't be afraid to give a clear 'no' to the activities other people would like to foist upon you, but which are not yours to carry

PREACHING – SUNDAY COMES AROUND EVERY WEEK

If you're part of any more organised expression of church, then this one event stands as central to the weekly rhythm of worship. We have not only put the preacher on a pedestal, but we have also done the same with the task itself. While you may wish to reshape the teaching process to allow for participation and interaction, chances are you will still be holding the floor and guiding the conversation.

In my early days of ministry, I felt acutely the pressure to preach well. Nothing was affirmed in our Baptist churches like good teaching, so I believed I could never turn up on Sunday with anything less than a 9.9/10 smokin' hot sermon. In those years, I regularly exceeded the sixteen hours of paid time I had available just to produce that sermon.

I experienced this pressure right up until my most recent role, when I decided that on weeks I was preaching, my sermon got eight hours. If it didn't come together in that time, then those present had to live with the fact that it was the best I could do. I have never been employed more than two days per week in the church over the last twelve years, so I have consciously tried to limit my preparation time to just one of those days.

I have discovered that if I do my best in eight hours then it's nearly always good enough. If I am speaking to people I know and love (as you can do in a smaller church) then *how* it is communicated matters as much as the content – to be able to adapt the stories to the people who are present, involve them in the discussion, and speak with clarity and conviction.

I have a hunch that if I spent another twenty or thirty hours on my sermons they may improve by ten or twenty per cent, but I'm *not* convinced that would be time well spent. In fact, I think the hours spent with people will usually prove to be of more value to my teaching than extra time immersed in books. I learnt this principle early in ministry as I watched a co-worker with low competence in the area of preaching. He was never criticised harshly, or brought undone for his uninspiring sermons, and this was simply because he really loved the people. His genuine love and concern for others saw his fairly pedestrian preaching overlooked and occasionally even enjoyed.

If you're bivocational and wondering how to manage your preaching load, my suggestion is to simply lower the bar.

Hear that again. *Lower the bar*!

Reduce the expectations you have of yourself. Realise that your congregation is not expecting you to be a world-class communicator, or to deliver your sermons from memory with polish and pizzazz. They can access world-class preaching on podcasts every day of the week. They just want you to be *yourself* and say something biblical, helpful and relevant to them honestly and understandably.

Here is some simple practical advice for effective communication from my own experiences as a bivocational pastor:

- **Know well in advance (at least four weeks ahead) what you will be preaching on.** Your brain can then subconsciously file relevant stories and ideas for use when you need them. Trust me – it works.
- **Break your preaching preparation in two.** Do some prep work early in the week. Research material, gather ideas and stories and then let them sit for a few days. Go to your other job. When you return to write the sermon later in the week, you will discover that the content you gathered earlier has not been sitting idle. The ideas that have been percolating in the back of your mind are now ready to use.
- **Allocate a specific amount of time to preparation and keep to your allocation.** Notice that you *can* get tasks completed in that time if you need to. Allow yourself the grace to present the best you have in the time available. For those who grew up in an environment that valued good preaching above all else, this will evoke withdrawal symptoms and anxiety. You may feel tetchy, worried that your teaching isn't good enough, that it lacks polish and finish. This may be true, but it is worth pushing through the 'withdrawals' to reach a healthier place.
- **Aim for personal connection over perfect content.** Your strength will likely be your relationship with the people in your

- congregation, rather than your hours spent in study. Tap into this and speak to those you know will be there, in a way you would if they visited your home.
- **Lower your expectations of yourself.** If preaching and/or communication is your gift, then expect to deliver an 8/10 sermon 8/10 weeks. On those other weeks, you may surprise yourself with a 9/10 or a 4/10. But if you can accept that it doesn't always go to plan you won't have a black day on Monday because of it. If it isn't your gift just remember that 5/10 is a pass…
- **Make sure you can summarise your message into one sentence that is relevant to your congregation**. It's not enough to articulate your one big idea. If that one big idea has no connection to your intended audience, then it will be clear but irrelevant. If you can describe *why* this message has currency, it will penetrate further into people's lives rather than simply being an academic exercise or a history lesson.
- **Let other people teach, and help them become strong communicators.** Use your other teachers, and help them develop their gift. I think it's reasonable to expect a full-time pastor to preach weekly, and maintain reasonable content and quality. If you are two or three days per week, I would suggest that fortnightly would be a more appropriate and sustainable rhythm unless your primary gift is teaching.

IF YOU HAVE TO HAVE MEETINGS

Many churches seem to love meetings, and the pastor's day can feel as though it is spent moving from one appointment to another. If your church is busy with much activity, it would be easy for a part-time staff member to spend the full allocation of paid hours attending prayer, leadership, and a range of other related team meetings. Some churches also have the rather unrealistic expectation that 'the pastor' will be present at every one of these meetings, so it will be important to establish clear boundaries and expectations early so that you can survive and the church is not disappointed.

Consider attending only the meetings where your presence is essential. Leave other capable people in charge of all others. You may discover that they need some training and development to lead their meetings well, but this is something worth investing time in. Rather than attending meetings and plugging the gap, you are always better served by teaching and training other leaders to do a better job.

If you have to lead a meeting, specify its purpose and plan the agenda accordingly. Some meetings only need to take fifteen minutes, while others may require a solid two-hour block. Let the purpose of the meeting frame the time allocated and the appropriate agenda. Management expert, Patrick Lencioni, comments that we tend to have one catch-all leadership meeting, meaning that we end up doing everything with mediocrity.[6] If you're a pastor with apostolic gifts then I'm sure you have sat in leadership meetings, wading through the administrivia while waiting for the 'big ideas' section of the agenda, only to realise that, for yet another month, the trivial has taken the lion's share of the participants' energy. If you only have time for one meeting then it is possible to arrange the agenda in such a way to reflect the team's priorities, but what is almost certain is that the urgent will always demand response, while the non-urgent, but important, will be put on hold yet again.

It is my own policy to ensure a meeting never runs longer than two hours, and that includes fifteen minutes of 'loose coffee time' at the start. When I hear of church meetings that run into the small hours of the morning I feel ill, as something has very likely gone drastically wrong when this is happening. No one makes well-informed decisions late at night when they are wishing they were in bed.

MANAGING EMERGENCIES

How do you respond if there is an emergency while you are working your other job and unavailable at that moment? A real problem with emergencies is that they can play on our desire to be needed. They can make us feel there is no one who can manage the situation quite like us.

In all likelihood, there are few real emergencies for which only a pastor can provide the solution. If you don't need to call 000 then it probably isn't an emergency. It may well be important, and the person making the call may sound distressed, but I would hazard a guess that the bulk of these calls could be served by support sources other than you. And if the church is functioning as it is supposed to, then there should be others in close contact with the person in question who can provide immediate support.

But if it *is* really a dire emergency? If someone is dying… or a marriage is about to dissolve … Then simply *do* everything in your power to be present and offer what help you can.

UNAVOIDABLE ADMINISTRIVIA

No matter what role you have in your church, you will inevitably have to deal with a certain amount of administration. Rosters, emails and risk assessments are just a few of the tasks a pastor may deal with. If you are wired administratively, then you will probably find great joy in organising rosters, managing budgets, and ensuring the church is compliant with government regulations. Someone has to do those tasks and, if you find joy in them, that's wonderful.

There are two traps we can fall into with admin work. The first danger is that your time can be easily swallowed up with these behind-the-scenes tasks. They provide a degree of satisfaction as each job is 'ticked off', but they have a tendency to consume much more time than they are worth. I have managed the church's website for several years, and I know I can easily blow half a day just trying to figure out bugs in the software. This is not what I am paid to do, so I now outsource complications to a professional, who will solve them in five or ten minutes. The second danger is that you can completely disregard the need for administrative competency. While we may have stumbled our way through in years gone by, the church now needs to be on top of its game in all areas, or it could find itself in an unwanted court case.

The simplest solution is either to find a committed volunteer, or to allocate resources to hiring an administrative worker. The mundane and generally less important work can be done by them, and you can focus on your areas of strength.

IF WE CAN'T DO IT?

If we can't do it then it doesn't get done. It's that simple. While this comes at the end of a long list of strategies for managing tasks, the ability to say a clear 'no' is vitally important. There is an endless list of 'good things' we could do as churches, projects to sign up for, charities to align with, conferences to attend, and ventures to pursue, but there is also the problem of finite people, time and resources. Not every good idea needs to be pursued, and some don't even need to be discussed.

If we can't staff it, we shut it down, no matter how valuable it may have been in days gone by. This is a really important strategy to use broadly, but not indiscriminately, as some things just can't be left undone. A treasurer pays the employees each month, as well as all bills, so we cannot get away without someone performing this task. However, many other projects are not critical to achieving our mission, and they can be closed down if we lack the resources.

FOR REFLECTION

- In the 5Q schema, which gift/s do you align most closely with, and how are you expressing these in your leadership?
- Consider the balance of your leadership team. Which gifts do your key leaders align with?
- Which gift is least represented in your leadership team?
- What tasks does the church *really* need you to perform?
- What is your process for recruiting people into ministry roles, and how effective is it?
- When preparing for preaching, are you able to do 'enough' and let it be, or do you need to continually strive for perfection? Why?
- What do you do to re-energise and to rest?
- How will you ensure that your meetings are needed, valuable, and run to time?
- What activities do you need to stop doing? What is preventing you from letting go of these?
- How can you build 'equipping for workplace mission' into the fabric of your church culture?

Notes

1. APEST = Apostle, prophet, evangelist, shepherd, teacher from Hirsch, A., *The Forgotten Ways*. (Brazos Grand Rapids, 2006)
2. http://www.theforgottenways.org/what-is-apest.aspx
3. You can complete an APEST assessment online here. https://missionalchallenge.com/apest-assessment
4. For an overview of Jesus' methodology see Coleman, R., *Master Plan of Evangelism* (Baker, Grand Rapids, 2010)
5. https://www.eisenhower.me/eisenhower-matrix
6. https://www.willmancini.com/blog/create-more-effective-meetings-with-4-types-of-structure

11

NAVIGATING THE COMPLEXITIES OF BIVOCATIONAL LIFE

When Danelle and I married, we already knew that I was the tidy one and she was the messy one. This became evident within a few days by the appearance of our bedroom. On my side of the bed was a bedside table with a lamp, a book and nothing else. On Danelle's bedside table were three magazines, three half-read books, a coffee mug, pens, jewelry, makeup, and much, much more… And then there was the clothing that had been strewn across the floor! When Mr Tidy married Miss Messy there were initially a few sparks as we tried to persuade each other to see the world from our point of view. In the end, we reached a compromise that worked for both of us. She would have the side of the bed away from the doorway so that her messiness would remain largely hidden and wouldn't disturb me. She could continue to be herself and I would continue to be myself. Problem solved.

But the fact remains that life is inherently messy, and we all approach it differently. No matter how much we attempt to snip the loose ends and tidy up the chaos, life has a way of surprising us. The bivocational life has the potential for great messiness and madness if it is approached the wrong way. However, if we can observe the complexity and then make conscious choices to manage the tensions, then chances are we will be able to live fruitfully, healthily, and even joyfully.

In bivocational leadership, various tensions and temptations can potentially conspire to bring us undone. It is possible, however, to be alert to what is ahead and therefore be equipped to manage these.

TENSIONS

TENSION 1. INTEGRATED VS SEPARATED?

Perhaps the first challenging question a bivocational pastor will face is: *To what extent will I seek to separate my work and church life, and to what extent will I allow them to overlap?*

Let's assume you work as a property manager for a real estate company three days of the week, and the church for two days. Here are some questions that you must be able to answer:

- *Do you have lunch with church folks on your property management days?*
- *Do you bring property management files home to process after hours and sometimes on church time?*
- *Do you ever 'trade' hours between the different roles, or do you clock on and clock off for both roles?*

Or you may be a teacher with a similar time distribution:

- *Do you ever do your marking or preparation on church days when you have spare time?*
- *Do you take school holidays as they are set, or do you engage in church work on those days?*
- *If your students were writing an exam, would you take time to do some back-end admin work for the church?*

I'm sure you can formulate your own questions of this kind. Some have clear answers, but the boundaries between roles can be murky and hard to pin down, meaning that we need to operate with wisdom and grace.

As a small business owner-operator, I have a huge degree of flexibility in how I manage my hours, and even my days. I have chosen to run my business Tuesday through Thursday, while making Mondays and Fridays available for church work in addition to the obligatory Sunday. But the often unpredictable nature of each role means that they frequently bleed into one another.

Danelle and I have adopted an integrated approach to the bivocational life as we have found this to be in keeping with who we are as people, and it sits better with a more holistic philosophy of ministry. It means that we intentionally allow the boundaries between roles to blur. We form our days purposefully, but also flexibly. Even within ministry itself, we have to make choices as to whether we are 'working' or just 'hanging out'. Sometimes that distinction is easy – for example, if we're involved in sermon preparation, or marriage counselling. If we invite people from church around for a meal then it becomes more complicated. We would rarely consider a meal with good friends from church to be part of our employment, as we are enjoying the time together and we haven't gathered for any work purposes.

I try to imagine Jesus living my life, and consider what He would view as 'work' or 'play', and it's hard – really hard – to see Jesus making a clear break. He simply lived His life and, along the way, He worked, played, ministered, and chose time away to recover and refresh.

I sense that an integrated approach may work well for certain personality types and stages of life. But for others, it makes sense to clearly delineate what, when and how this division of labour will occur. If you are planning to enter the bivocational arena, you may want to consider which approach will best serve you, before you find yourself overwhelmed and faced with demands from all sides. Neither approach is perfect – but one approach may well be better suited to you and your family at this stage of your life.

TENSION 2. MANAGING EXPECTATIONS

When it comes to how we engage in ministry, we find ourselves confronted with a diverse set of expectations from various stakeholders:

- **Our Church Leaders** – When we were employed our leaders expected us to perform certain tasks, and work in ways that were in keeping with the culture of the church. Some of those expectations were clear at the interview, but some were either assumed or implied and inevitably needed working out at a later point.
- **The 'Church'** – That is every bit as nebulous as it sounds. Who is 'the church'? Ideally, it will be a shared communal expectation, but more often than not the church is the conglomeration of many people's experience of pastors and church cultures over many years. It is complicated because many expectations are simply personal preferences of how a pastor should work and behave.

- **Spouse** – If you are married, you will hopefully have talked with your spouse about the form your bivocational life will take, and you will agree on certain parameters to ensure there is adequate time for healthy family life. There will also need to be ongoing conversations about how things are panning out.
- **Church Staff** – In a multi-staff church, you will need to have expectations of each other, and these will need to be communicated clearly to avoid misunderstanding or ill feelings.
- **You** – You enter ministry with thoughts about how it should develop, and you will imagine yourself performing certain tasks with competency. We rarely have low expectations of ourselves, and it's often the excessively demanding self-imposed expectations that can be our undoing.

These are just five immediate sources of expectation. We could also consider denominational requirements if your church is wired that way, or you may be influenced by the expectations of peers in ministry who are keen to see how this 'bivocational thing' works for you. Additionally, you are likely to have expectations from your employer, workmates, clients or customers.

Edington identifies two key questions that help shape expectations within a church community:

> *Two simple questions turned out to be the most powerful tools available to us in helping us understand how that old culture worked and how we might change it. The questions were "What do you expect the pastor to do?" and "How necessary is it for a pastor to do that?"*[1]

Traditional models of church see the pastor performing the primary liturgical and care-based tasks, with higher churches needing more clergy involvement than lower churches. However, for the bivocational pastor, there needs to be a willingness to devolve some of the usual pastoral responsibilities to the members of the church. It will primarily be the role of the pastor to help this process happen. Pastors who need to be in control of every ministry, or feel no one will do the job quite like them, are just not suited to a bivocational life, as they are unable to surrender some of what they view as significant. This inevitably leads to overload, burn out, and disappointment for both pastor and congregation.

For most of us, the expectations we impose on ourselves are harsher and more demanding than anything external. We can afford to be kinder to ourselves and, for our wellbeing and longevity, it's certainly worth doing so.

TENSION 3. WHO AM I TODAY?

As a pastor, you inevitably find yourself in various roles that give flavour to your leadership. My youth ministry days coincided with a period of life when I was coaching a lot of basketball and athletics, so it was as if the coach persona carried over into the church arena when I tried to form a team who would perform at their best.

Pastors function in various modes; some as managers, some as generals, and others like farmers, to name just a few. Until recently, I told people that I felt as though I had been taking on the role of 'dad', the fatherly head of the home. I seemed to be the person who made others feel safe, as well as being the one who carried the primary weight of responsibility for the family. I identified with Paul in 2 Corinthians 11:28 where he wrote: 'Besides everything else, I face daily the pressure of my concern for all the churches'. And, in 1 Corinthians 4:15, he writes 'you have many teachers but few fathers' (few parental types who will love and care with patience). I would never have dreamt this possible in my adventurous, younger years, as I had wanted to be all about shaking things up and pursuing new initiatives.

In the last few years I have observed the need to change again. During the writing of this book I swapped roles with our other pastors, and I am now serving as an associate pastor while the younger guys have stepped up to lead. At this point, 'dad' no longer feels like the best metaphor to describe my contribution. And I am sensing a sort of 'tribal elder' identity forming in its place. This speaks of a different approach yet again. I am intentionally less visible as a leader, but still present and available as needed. My hope is to remain as a keeper of the cultural DNA of our churches and as a support to the younger men and women who are leading in different areas.[2]

If you can articulate the shape of your leadership, and if you can assign a description to that role, then chances are you will be much more effective. You won't be trying to function as CEO, coach and parent all at once, nor will you be wearing a general's uniform when you should really be wearing a farmer's overalls.

TENSION 4. PRACTICING CONTENTMENT

A few years ago I visited my physiotherapist, who happened to have a work experience student with him in the room. I'd been seeing Damian for ten years, and we know each other reasonably well. But I was unprepared for the way he introduced me to his student.

Looking at me curiously, he said: "Alana, this is… Andrew". Damian paused as he hesitated in describing my life. He then chose two words I would never have entertained. "He's… semi-retired."

I said nothing. I wasn't up for explaining my life and vocational choices to Alana the work experience girl, and I doubted she'd care to hear them either. But Damian *knew* me. He was fully aware that I run my irrigation and turf business three days a week and that I pastor a church for the other two.

Yet he still introduced me as semi-retired.

Every time I think about this I chuckle. How did he arrive at this descriptor? Perhaps to him, that is how my life appears, or maybe I *am* semi-retired and I just don't know it? I'm certainly not in any position to officially retire in the near future, and I have no intention of ever retiring as we understand it in our culture.

I sense that what Damian has observed over the years is less to do with the quantity of work I do, and more about the mindset I bring to my roles. I have a dark history of workaholism in my twenties and thirties, and a determination never to return there. So these days I aim to work at approximately 70% capacity. Yeah, that's right – 70%. It's not a huge number, is it? But if I operate well at 70% capacity then I can complete everything that needs to be done without wearing out.

70% is sustainable.

70% has margin for those days when nothing goes to plan.

70% means I am rarely rushing, and I'm a nicer person to be around.

As I read the gospels, I see Jesus living purposefully, but I find it hard to imagine Him packing His days with back-to-back appointments. He always seemed to have time to stop and be present with people. He rarely appeared to be in a hurry, and I am sure that was a conscious choice. I believe that operating this way will mean I am still going when I'm eighty-five years old. I may be a bit slower, but hopefully continuing with purpose and passion.

As a bivocational worker, the great challenge is to complete enough tasks to keep things moving, without overworking in either job. The reality is that if you are employed for two days by the church, but actually work four, you still won't move forwards at the speed of someone who works six days, or two full-time employees, or a team of ten full-time employees. But, no matter how much gets done, there will always be *more* to do. Hear that. There is A L W A Y S more to do. The alternative is to learn contentment – to learn how to release the need to control, achieve and be seen to succeed. If you're achievement-driven, then life in bivocational ministry may well frustrate you because, just as you gain traction on a project or an initiative, you have to put it down until next week. And when next week comes around, it does so with its own fresh challenges.

In Philippians 4, Paul writes of learning to be content with his physical circumstances 'whether in need or in plenty'. In that vein, I sense that whether we are bivocational or in full-time in ministry, we need to learn *contentment* with our circumstances. We can never do all there is to do. And, if we ever feel as though we are getting to the bottom of our to-do list, we will soon find more. The operative idea in this section of scripture is one of *learning* – of somehow appreciating that, wherever we find ourselves, we are able to grow into the ability to be content and at peace.

When we live within our means, we resist scheduling a new activity every term just to be seen to be busy and effective. We aren't driven by the approval of the imaginary voices in our heads. We sometimes do little, or even just enough, knowing that when the Spirit calls us, we may have to run hard for an extended period – and that is ok too.

To that end it has been said that we need to focus less on time management and more on energy management, recognising that we have periods of productivity, and then times when we struggle to focus or complete tasks.

I know that my most productive times are first thing in the morning. If I have a sermon to write or important 'brain work' to do, I will attack it early when I can give it my best. I can use evenings for the kind of pastoral work that probably looks like sitting by a fire with friends. And it is that... except it's also purposeful.

TENSION 5. JOB/CAREER/FAMILY – WHAT IS THIS THING ANYWAY?

There are few jobs as complicated as that of a local church pastor, and the bivocational dimension adds another layer of complexity. In one breath we speak of our church as family, and in the next as our job and profession. We intend to be a community of unconditional love and acceptance but, when it comes time for a performance review, we may discover that we have been voted out of the tribe due to a below-par ministry effort.

Kent Carlson writes:

> *The best metaphor for church community is the healthy family, not the marketplace. It is psychologically damaging for a spouse or child to live in a home where a certain level of performance is required for the relationship to be valued.*[3]

I couldn't agree more. Yet the reality is that, for many pastors, the church is *not* just their family. There *is* a baseline level of performance that must be attained if money is to change hands – and this is not unreasonable. Even for the most stable, dedicated and long-term pastors, the presence of money in the relationship means that it is always going to cause them to 'perform', rather than simply being part of the family.

In addition to the challenge of navigating the family versus job tension, many church roles involving relationships and physical presence, also expect that the pastor will live in or close to the suburb in which the church is based. For many families, this involves uprooting their previous life and relationships to move and start again. The church then becomes not only the new family but also the employer, a strange and sometimes tense combination.

With employment regulations and conditions being what they are, it's impossible not to regard pastors as employed staff, but the challenge will always be to find ways of creating a culture that blends the best of family, with the best of the protection and clarity that a job contract supplies.

Of course, if we add the notion of career into this already complicated relationship, we end up with another layer of complexity. I simply can't imagine Jesus ever speaking of a 'career in ministry'. This language would never have entered His vocabulary, but the professionalisation of ministry means that this is now a genuine consideration for many pastors. But be warned, the further a pastor moves down the career pathway, the further he or she moves away from the church as family.

The challenge is always to ensure the language we use when speaking of church and ministry is language that we could easily locate in the pages of scripture.

TENSION 6. IS SUNDAY A WORK DAY?

If you are employed two days per week by a church, should your participation on Sunday be considered part of your working hours? After thirty years of working as a pastor, I'm yet to know the answer to this question. Some part-time pastors I have spoken to work two weekdays as well as Sunday, while others work one day during the week in addition to Sunday. Different churches have had various (unwritten) policies, and few have articulated them clearly.

Unless your church has a definite policy, my suggestion is to simply do what feels right for you. As with most issues in church life, communication is the key. Making sure people are on the same page allows for minimal misunderstanding and ill-feeling. If your predecessor counted Sunday as part of their total hours, then chances are you will be able to, but if they set aside two weekdays for work, you may find yourself working with a congregation whose views are already set in that direction.

TENSION 7. HOURS VS OUTCOMES?

In my irrigation business, I am often asked to provide an estimate of how much a job will cost before starting. Once we agree on a price my goal is not to work a specific number of hours, but simply to complete the job properly. It may take me ten hours or it may take me twenty, but what matters is the quality of the outcome. This is my preferred way to view church work too. I am paid to lead, teach, and meet with men. If I can demonstrate that I have done these things well over the course of a week, then the total hours spent is less important.

My preference at this point in my life is to operate in church as I do in business, and lean in the direction of achieving specific outcomes, rather than working for a set period of time. In the early years of ministry, I was employed for two days and it took me at least that time to write a sermon. Everything else I was expected to do happened outside of that time. These days I am faster at preparing sermons. I am also less of a perfectionist when it comes to communication, so I will never burn sixteen hours on this one task.

I also know that some weeks require more of me than others, so I allow myself to go hard for a week, and work at a slower pace the following week. In a previous era, I would have clocked a minimum of sixteen hours every week and then worked extra hours unpaid. We have occasionally taken the step of keeping timesheets to document our working hours but, in our church culture, where we allow work and friendship lines to blur, these always became difficult to maintain with any degree of accuracy.

Whatever approach is used, it needs to be understood and agreed to by the church leaders, so that awkward questions aren't later raised as to whether you are doing your job.

Every system is open to abuse, but the hope is that pastors are not unscrupulous enough to dodge their responsibilities. The key is to operate with grace and wisdom, recognising that different situations require different responses.

TENSION 8. RESTING LOOKS DIFFERENT FOR EVERYONE

To have a sustainable ministry we must figure out how to rest well, and that is often easier said than done. Jesus modelled the practice of rest by regularly calling His disciples away from the crowds and into a place of renewal. The practice of at least one day off each week has been essential for ongoing health. One of the real challenges of being bivocational is to take that day without feeling guilty for it. My diligence in this practice needed to be more rigid in the early years of ministry when I was highly driven but, in more recent years, I have allowed a greater degree of fluidity, so I am less an advocate of a strict sabbath.

In Mark 6:30-34, we see Jesus with a group of weary disciples who needed a rest, so He tried to get them away to a quiet place where they could get some respite from the crowds. They jumped in their boat to head for what Mark described as a 'solitary place' only to realise that, as they arrived, the people had got wind of their destination and were already there to meet them. Rather than becoming angry and frustrated at this intrusion on His downtime, Jesus had compassion on them because they were like sheep without a shepherd. Rather than resting He sat down and began to teach them.

Depending on whose ministry formation school you went through, you may want to critique Jesus for His lax boundaries, or you may just want to commend Him on His ability to flex and sacrifice His own rest and recovery.

The point is that there is no law about how resting should be done. If Jesus could break the R & R code from time to time, perhaps we should see that as a sign that we can too, so long as we clearly understand that this is what we are doing. I am not advocating sloppy boundaries and poor people management. Rather it's a challenge to operate within the spirit of the sabbath rather than adhering to it as a rigid law.

A few years ago, I was interviewed for a short video at a pastors' conference where the theme was 'Returning to the Well', a metaphor for coming back to Jesus as our source of energy and inspiration. When the interviewer asked me how I 'return to the well' as a bivocational pastor, I responded by saying that instead of returning to the well, I now try to 'live by the well'. By this, I meant living an intentionally simple, slow-paced and spacious life that allows time for regular reflection and connection with God. I said it without much thought, but I later realised that I had been learning something really valuable about my connection with the Spirit.

As a bivocational pastor living in a busy world, there will always be the temptation to squeeze extra tasks into the day. However, the reality is that no matter how much we do, there will always be more to be done. The work of the church will never be complete until Jesus returns, so our responsibility is to manage our time in such a manner that we are faithful to the mission in a sustainable and healthy way

I now view success as being in control of my life, rather than living on the ragged edge and dodging breakdowns and marriage dust-ups. I have a friend who tells me he would rather burn out than rust out, and I think I probably would too if those were the only options on the table. The reality is that no one expects us to do either. In fact, what our church needs from us is a working model of healthy living where there is ample time for work activities, family, recreation, and relationships. Pastors, who are always busy and on the brink of a breakdown, are not living a life that represents Jesus well, and they need to be encouraged to slow down and reflect more carefully on what is happening, and why.

TENSION 9. WHEN YOU HATE YOUR OTHER JOB

Ok so let's be brutally honest…

Occasionally the only thing keeping you in work is the need to provide income for your family. If you are in this place and finding your work tedious and unrewarding, perhaps the first thing you need to hear is that sometimes *this is enough*. There are moments when you just have to suck it up and press on, because there are bills to pay and no one else is going to do it for you. Sorry if you were hoping for a reason to quit. I can't give you one if you have no other job to go to.

Those of us in affluent countries live with a certain degree of privilege, believing that we should be able to enjoy our work and find deep personal fulfilment there. I agree that *ideally* this would be the case – that our jobs would be joyful, meaningful, and purposeful. But there are times when work is hard, or we lose interest, and we simply need to turn up and earn the money. When we do this as bivocational pastors, we model faithfulness and perseverance to others whose jobs may also be unfulfilling.

If your workplace is unsafe, if there is bullying or abuse, then obviously those issues need addressing. If there is no resolution then perhaps your resignation may be the only option, but these are the more exceptional circumstances. The problems most of us face are more likely to be related to boredom or disinterest, and having to push ourselves to complete tasks we don't enjoy. When I'm talking to people in this space, I usually encourage them to take what I call the Balinese Taxi Driver test. These guys start work at 7.00 am and often finish late at night, only to repeat the whole thing the next day. They do so because they know that if they don't work, their families don't eat. A driver might dream of opening an art studio, or being a software engineer, but at the end of the day, there are bills to pay. I simply ask: "If he can do that for his family, then surely you can deal with a bit of boredom behind the checkout, or on the shop floor?"

FOR REFLECTION

As you move forward some key issues to reflect on and discuss would be:

- Are you likely to take a more integrated or separate approach to ministry and work? Why would you choose this direction, and what will be its strengths and weaknesses?
- If shared expectations are critical to a healthy bivocational ministry, then how would you deal with the following questions?
    - How often will the pastor preach?
    - What happens with pastoral care if the pastor is not available?
    - Which meetings does the pastor need to attend?
    - What course of action will be taken if there is a pastoral need on the pastor's non-church day?
    - What (if anything) is expected of the pastor's spouse?
- What does it mean for you to 'live within your means, and what changes may this necessitate in your life?
- What language do you generally use to describe your pastoral role, and what impact does this have on how you operate day by day?
- Will you consider Sunday a work day? Why, or why not?

- Do you prefer hours, or outcomes, to measure what you have been doing at work? Why?
- Earlier I mentioned that I have at times played the roles of coach, 'dad', and tribal elder. What role do you play in your church, and how does knowing this shape your leadership practices?

Notes

[1] Edington, Mark D. W., *Bivocational*. (Kindle Locations 801-803). Church Publishing Inc. Kindle Edition.
[2] 'Churches' is plural because we serve at our original church (Quinns Baptist) as well as the church we planted (Yanchep Community Church)
[3] Kent Carlson; Mike Lueken, *Renovation of the Church: What Happens When a Seeker Church Discovers Spiritual Formation.* (Kindle Locations 882-883). Kindle Edition.

12

IF THE FUTURE IS BIVOCATIONAL...

We're queued up in peak hour traffic, waiting for the right-hand turn signal at one of Perth's slowest intersections. My son, Sam, is sitting next to me. He is on holiday and helping me out with some irrigation work.

"Hey, Dad, it won't be long until we have driverless cars!" he says.

"Driverless cars – sounds weird," I reply.

"Yeah, well, it's comin'..."

"Will we have automated traffic lights?" I ask. "How will they deal with roundabouts? If one bit of software glitches does that means thousands die?" I have questions – lots of them. I can't easily imagine a world with driverless cars. Besides, I like driving, and I'm not keen to hand over that enjoyment to a robot.

"It's coming, Dad. Just need to get ready. One day you will be able to sit and read a book while the car takes you to your next job."

THE FUTURE IS BIVOCATIONAL

Maybe the future looks very different to our current experience, and perhaps driverless cars will be safer, faster, and more reliable than anything manned by people. But I have trouble wrapping my head around the idea. I have trouble even wanting it to happen. I like things as they are.

I wonder if this isn't how it is for those of us who have been in the church a long time, and have come to like the familiar and the predictable? We *like* a full-time pastor who preaches, inspires, and rallies the troops. This is what we have always known, and it feels safe, so it may be something of an unknown to suggest a church could be led by bivocational staff, where members are required to have a much greater and more significant contribution.

Questions emerge immediately. What if there is a funeral on a day the pastor is working their other job? What if an emergency counselling situation develops, and we can't contact the pastor? Are we *really* going to share the preaching? Won't that risk us being exposed to heretical teaching by untrained preachers?

There are plenty more questions to field, but I am also sure that, if a church is committed to a new vision of embracing bivocational pastors and greater involvement from the congregation, then those questions will be resolved. Someone else will take the funeral. We can recommend an off-site counsellor. The chances of someone feeling brave enough to test out their heretical theological views on the congregation are minimal. Most new preachers typically play it very safe.

If envisaging a bivocational future is difficult for you or your church, there are a number of approaches that could help shift rusted-on imaginations.

■ TRY IT!

In speaking of incarnational mission, Alan Hirsch once stated: "We have to act ourselves into a new way of thinking". We have to start the process of 'doing the stuff', in the belief that it will be effective, even if our default settings are stuck within an old framework. But as we practice new ways, we begin to rewire neural pathways, and we learn how to do this new thing well. Action is integral to creating a new reality. If all we do is ponder, plan and pontificate, we will most likely still be pondering five years later.

You don't need to reorganise the whole church to have someone on your team operating bivocationally. Chances are that many churches already have pastors operating in this way, but the value of their other vocation has not been acknowledged, nor mined for its value to both pastor and church. Perhaps you could begin by encouraging staff members to discuss their work experiences. Through a supervision or coaching process, help them identify the opportunities God has placed in front of them, both inside *and* outside the church realm.

In interviews for future part-time appointments, it would be beneficial to speak with candidates about their other work, and how they envisioned this operating in sync with the ministry role. You could take the time to encourage them to regard this as more than just their 'side hustle', but rather a legitimate and valuable vocational choice. If they know that they will be sent and supported as a workplace missionary as well as a pastor, it may change the way they view the role. So instead of apologising for only being able to offer part time work, you can speak boldly of your church's vision for a team of bivocational pastors, and communicate that this approach is intentional and purposeful. The flip side of being upfront in your support of an intentional bivocational role is that you will also be communicating to the applicant that there is no promise of their role becoming full-time if the church grows.

If you are a pastor wanting to move in this direction, a simple way to begin might be to commit half a day, or a full day, per week to start a small business, or pick up a local job. You may be able to start something new without having to stop your full-time role. If you share this vision with your leadership team they may even free you to pursue other work, while on a full-time salary, in the expectation that the outcome will be fruitful and beneficial to both church and pastor.

But don't leave it untried just because it's complicated. Move towards becoming bivocational, share your hopes with your church leaders and, when the time is right, take a step of faith and attempt something new. What's the worst that can happen?

TEACH IT

I don't remember ever hearing a single class on the value of bivocational mission and ministry during my time in theological education. I know many colleges offered 'streams' for those who wanted to specialise in different aspects of ministry, such as youth work, team leadership, or worship ministry. Perhaps a 'bivocational' stream could be introduced or, at very least, a unit that equips students to think like missionaries in their workspace, as well as preparing them for a distinctly bivocational ministry position.

Some leave their workplaces to follow the call of God into ministry. Often that severing is so clear and final that to return, in any way, feels like a betrayal of calling. But I sense that part of the reason for this is because we have been conditioned to 'hear the call' to 'drop our nets' and follow – to head off to seminary to be equipped for a new career. But I'm curious as to what it meant for Peter and John, and whether it was a permanent and complete separation, or if it was more fluid.

So there's a challenge for the theological educators – to prepare people for 'ministry +' and to equip them to deal positively with the reality that there are only so many full-time pastoral roles. Increasingly, pastors will be working second jobs but, if approached with bivocational intent and missional savvy, that second job can be much more than a way to pay the bills.

TEAM UP

Let me imagine for a moment that you are a solo pastor reading this book, and thinking it would be great to have another vocational expression outside of the local church. You believe that this could be valuable for both you and your people. But rather than stopping there, why not dream *with* your leadership team about forming a crew of bivocational staff, who each serve in different ways to meet the various needs that your church has.

You already know you can't do it all yourself. This is a way you can diversify your staff, and form a team-based primarily around the Ephesians 4 gift paradigm. A church that is willing to accept the challenge could reinvent itself with a team who fill the apostle, prophet, evangelist, pastor, teacher roles. This would be a far healthier outcome than employing one person who serves as 'pastor' irrespective of his or her actual gifting.

The future will be increasingly bivocational, and the place to start for existing staff teams is to begin imagining what new possibilities exist for those who are currently full-time. A team that approaches this together can support one another in the challenges of transitioning away from the mindset and practice of a church led by a full-time pastor. You can also help the congregation embrace the new paradigm.

I realise that may sound a whole lot easier than it actually is. But why not at least try it? Begin to move in that direction, trusting that the God who holds the Universe in His care can see you and bless your endeavours.

PERSIST

I believe that the future *is* bivocational for churches in the Western world. This is already the everyday reality for many of our brothers and sisters in the developing world who have no other choice. If we can dispense with our privileged expectation of a fully-funded pastoral role, we can begin to imagine a different way of being.

I have already suggested plenty of ways to tackle that transition. What I can't do is give you a strategy for persistence and long-term success. Some days you just have to dig in, believe in what you are doing, and keep moving.

You learn perseverance by *persevering*. If you quit too soon, you simply become proficient in quitting. Your character and resolve weakens. If you tough it out, you develop inner strength and fortitude. You build character as you practice grit and determination – as you refuse to quit.

At times, it will be rewarding and invigorating, but on other occasions it will feel like wading through mud, and you will want to walk away.

Just don't.

Instead in those moments, choose to reflect on:

- the conversations you've had in the workplace that you would never at church;
- the people you now have relationships with who don't consider themselves part of your congregation;
- what you are learning as a missionary in a new context; and
- the new life you are immersed in, and the opportunities to live and speak about the kingdom of God.

When you have finished reflecting you will give thanks for the opportunities you would have missed out on had your life been contained solely within the church community.

WHO'S COMING WITH ME?

I think *Jerry Maguire* may be one of my all time favourite movies. A jaded but successful sports agent, with more clients than he can manage, suddenly does a stocktake on the shape of his life and, in a night of frightening revelation, writes what he calls his 'mission statement', appropriately titled

'The things we think and do not say'. It is a complete rejection of his existing modus operandi, and a vision of how sports agents could better serve their clients.

The answer was going to be *fewer* clients, *less money* and *more* personal attention. It was a beautiful dream – a moment of calling back to what a sports agent really ought to be – one who looks after the best interests of the player, rather than a salesman who sees people as just another dollar sign destined for exploitation.

As his mission statement is read by those in his office, Jerry's purist dream is quietly mocked by other staff. He decides it is time to draw a line in the sand. So he stands and announces his exit from the company. As he does, he shares his vision for a better way of working and boldly calls: "Who's coming with me?" The response is utterly underwhelming as no one moves or speaks. His personal assistant declines as she has a pay rise imminent. Eventually office girl, Dorothy Boyd, stands and states: "I will come with you". She chooses to walk out with Jerry into an unknown and unpredictable future, to be his new personal assistant.

Occasionally when I talk with pastors, I feel like they are in a Jerry Maguire type situation. They have lost faith in the system they are part of, they believe there is a better way to live and serve the kingdom of God, but the challenge they face is to: a) imagine a new way of doing life and church; and b) have the courage to step out into the unknown.

There comes a point where you have to choose a different path. More of the same inputs will inevitably result in more of the same outputs. Perhaps *you* need to make a stand, and chart a new course in your own life and ministry. Throughout this book, I have advocated for the bivocational option, to be considered as the staple form of leadership for neighbourhood churches in years to come for a number of core reasons:

1. Missional Effectiveness. If pastors in 'secular' jobs can recalibrate their imagination to see the potential for mission in their workplaces, perhaps they will be better able to equip the church for its mission in this sphere of life.

When a pastor's focus is on developing the internal workings of the church, and growing its numbers, it may be because he or she has not yet figured out how to teach and equip people for workplace mission.

Most churches are still highly Sunday-centric, and much of the pastor's time and energy is given to making the Sunday event operate more effectively. This 'centre' is reinforced by a consumer culture that dictates that Sundays should be inspiring and easy to access. However, the future missional effectiveness of the church will not be shaped around the attractiveness of the Sunday gathering, or the whims of fickle consumers. Instead, it will be built on a foundation of people taught, equipped, and empowered to serve outside of the church environment, while being supported by their church community every step of the way.

2. Healthier Churches. When a church is led by a 'pastor' it is done so by a person with one, or perhaps two, primary gifts. The pastor may be a 'pastor/teacher', or a 'prophet/evangelist' or an 'apostle/teacher', but no single person will ever embody all of the gifts and capacities needed for a healthy church.

However, churches that have chosen to operate within a bivocational framework may replace one pastor with two, or maybe even three. In doing so, they can potentially include the full complement of gifts in the leadership. A balanced, healthy church will be better equipped to serve its community than a church with a narrower focus.

A church of this form will also require its members to step up and participate fully in the life of the church, rather than relying on paid staff to do the heavy lifting. This may be a learning curve for everyone, as pastors release control and members assume more responsibility. In doing so, perhaps the church can better embody the priesthood of all believers instead of the select few.

3. Sustainability. In years ahead we will need to seriously rethink how we call people to contribute financially to the work of the church. A church solely dependent on congregational contributions may struggle. Shifts in giving patterns, accompanied by a consumer culture that encourages a user-pays approach, means that supporting pastors solely based on member income will be increasingly problematic.

Further complicating this is the potentially compromising effect of a full-time salary. Pastors have always known about this, and have simply attempted to faithfully negotiate the challenges. But the reality is that when a church is staffed by one person whose salary depends on the contributions of those church members, then that staff member may be less likely to challenge the congregation about areas of cultural idolatry. If a pastor is not solely reliant on the community for his or her weekly wage, it is more likely that he or she will speak about hot issues with more conviction and less fear.

4. Necessity – We Will Have No Choice. Someone once said: 'Necessity is the mother of invention'.[11] It may well be that necessity is the key driver behind a shift towards bivocational mission and ministry. We have a habit of resisting change, until the pain of staying put outweighs the pain of stepping into the new initiative.

I imagine this is how we will move forward.

---

[1] Loosely ascribed to Plato https://www.dictionary.com/browse/necessity-is-the-mother-of-invention

EMBRACE THE OPPORTUNITY

The future of the church in the Western world looks increasingly polarised.

As previously mentioned, I predict that the larger mega-church franchises will continue to grow and expand their reach, absorbing some of the smaller communities, as well as merging with other churches of similar ilk. They will continue to run large, inspiring gatherings intended to attract people into their orbit, while relying on smaller group structures for the relational connections people need to truly feel they are part of the church. When done extremely well, the attractional mode of mission can be effective and, perhaps in the years ahead, the sparseness of these churches will see them offer something relatively unique.

Their Achilles heel will always be the dance with consumer culture, as they navigate the challenge of discipling people to 'die to self' while being told that next week will be bigger and better and 'you won't want to miss it'. Some will be able to live with this tension and lead within it, but it will always be a balancing act. No doubt there will be some part-time staff employed by these churches, but their challenge will be to fully embrace their bivocational status while the centripetal force of the church draws their focus ever inward.

For pastors who cannot find their way within larger, event-focused churches, the option is to lead a smaller church and embrace their bivocational status as a privilege rather than a burden. Here there is potential for a significant number of churches to purposefully choose to reinvent, not just how they do Sunday, but how they do *everything*. While this change may be forced on some, others will recognise the need early and implement these adjustments sooner rather than later.

As always, it will be the brave few who chart a new course, and choose to risk failure in their pursuit of a creative way of being the church. If you are already bivocational, you are perfectly positioned to help the church with this transition. Even if you are grudgingly bivocational, it only takes a shift in mindset to embrace a new purpose in your workplace, and to see the insights you can share with your church community as you seek to be a workplace missionary.

I hope this book has inspired you to consider the enormous missional possibilities of the bivocational life, and that it has encouraged you to reflect deeply on both your role in the 'body' and the nature and shape of this thing we call 'church'.

I am convinced the future is bivocational. Embrace it, and step into it, making the most of every opportunity that comes your way, and may the church of Jesus Christ be stronger, and more effective than ever as we move forward into this new era.

FOR REFLECTION

- If the bivocational approach isn't already part of your church life, how may you create space to 'try it'?
- If some of your church staff are already bivocational by necessity, how may you help them sharpen their focus so that it becomes intentional and purposeful rather than just an income stream?
- Imagine you are speaking to your church leaders about bivocational ministry as an intentional strategy for moving forward in a secular culture. What key points do you hope will persuade your leaders to pursue this path?
- What would be the major obstacles to a bivocational approach in your church context? How might you navigate these?
- If you haven't already done so, list the names of people with whom you could purposefully share the bivocational journey, encouraging and inspiring one another along the way.
- If someone asked you for one major takeaway from this book what would it be?

Notes

1. Loosely ascribed to Plato https://www.dictionary.com/browse/necessity-is-the-mother-of-invention

EPILOGUE

It's nearing four o'clock on a chilly midwinter afternoon and my son, Sam, has just arrived home from school. Having seen the rising swell, he is eager to surf one of our local breaks, a gnarly, difficult wave that he has never attempted before. I have surfed it just twice, and felt out of my depth on both occasions.

I too had checked the swell earlier in the day, and I know there are sizable waves waiting for those brave enough to enter the water. I am not one of those people, but my sixteen-year-old son is determined to paddle out and take his place in the lineup. On one hand, my chest fills with pride at his courage and willingness to take on a wave that can be brutal and intimidating. Yet I feel anxiety, partly for him but also because I wonder whether I should be paddling out with him.

I note that it will be 4.15 pm at best by the time he gets in the water. The sun goes down at 5.00 pm, so it will be pitch black by 5.45 pm.

"Are you sure you're up for it and able to handle it?" I look him in the eye to check his resolve. "It will be your first time surfing this wave."

"Yeah, I'm keen!" he says, not really answering my question.

I know he wants to push himself and to place himself in situations that stretch his capacity, so I'm pleased with his unflinching response.

"Ok grab your gear and we'll head down," I respond quickly.

There comes a time in a boy's life when he needs to attempt some of these challenging, fear-inducing activities, so I'm not going to discourage him. I do want to be there to share it with him though, so I find a warm jacket as he slides into his wetsuit. It's a two-minute drive to the beach, and we chatter nervously on the way there. I'm not sure if it's him or me who is most tense.

As we pull into the car park, I see Tom's old army jeep parked up. It's a distinctive and easily recognisable car in our local area. (Remember Tom – my client with cancer who I wrote about in the introduction?) Tom is a 'waterman', someone who has been around the ocean his whole life. He has surfed some very challenging waves, so this is just a mellow end to a workday for him. Seeing Tom's car means my own anxiety drops a couple of notches because I am confident Tom will look out for Sam and ensure he stays safe. I am immediately grateful for good men like Tom.

We park the car and jog over the dunes, just in time to see a large wave break far out to sea, detonating on a small tribe of surfers who have positioned themselves too close to shore.

"Seeya, Dad," Sam yells as he heads down to the water. "Oh… Where do I paddle out?"

This is critical information. I point to the gap in the reef, and he gives me the thumbs up. I'm glad his mum isn't here to watch this.

He paddles out strongly, and makes it to the back of the lineup without any trouble. I lock my eyes on him, making sure I don't lose sight of him. Any number of things could go wrong. One massive set could wash him over the reef and into trouble. He could be held down by consecutive large waves, become trapped in an underwater cave or snap a leg rope. That said,

EPILOGUE

I don't have a plan for how I might help. I am just there, watching my son taking every young surfer's rite of passage – paddling out in waves that are well out of his comfort zone. I too have been here, albeit many years ago, and I remember the jelly legs and butterflies in the stomach as I tried to convince myself it would be ok.

Sam sits in the pack for a long time without catching a wave. To be fair, no one is. It's a tricky break at the best of times, and today the shifting swell has made it even harder. Tom drops in on a couple, but he is finding it difficult too. I jog back to the car to retrieve my phone, and upon my return only four small black dots are visible in the water, when previously there were five.

None of them look like Sam. My gut churns. Where is he? The sun is low on the horizon, so he has either been caught inside by a large wave and rolled towards shore, or he has given up and found his way in.

Just ten minutes later and those exiting the water have all walked past me. Sam is not amongst them. I figure he *must* still be out there, but I can't see him. I am becoming more worried by the minute. The sun is close to setting, and I am wishing he would paddle in. I also know that sometimes the journey to shore can be difficult when huge waves are at your back. I mutter a frustrated prayer and wait, hoping he will soon appear.

I suddenly catch sight of his form again. He was there all the time, but I couldn't recognise him. There is now just one other surfer with him in the water as the sun sets. The other surfer is Tom, and he is sitting close to Sam. My nerves ease; I know Tom will not leave Sam alone to find his way in through the darkness. Tom will guide him back to shore.

The sun sets further. Neither Sam nor Tom have made a move towards shore. More than likely the conversation sounds like: "One more and I'm outta here…" But it is almost dark and the car park crowd has all but disappeared. The passage back to shore is the same as the one out, between an opening in a particular section of reef. Missing that gap can result in a nasty pounding on the reef itself.

In the rush to enter the water, I hadn't explained to Sam that he needed to paddle back in through the same gap. Again, I hope that Tom will steer him to safety. As the last light disappears, I see that Sam and Tom are paddling towards the opening in the reef. I can't hear a word, of course, but I am almost certain Tom is encouraging my son for his courage, instead of focusing on the waves he didn't catch. Tom is cheering Sam on for being brave enough to paddle out. He is clearly guiding Sam back to shore. Tom is ensuring my son is safe. As they reach the reef, Tom points to the way in and waits until Sam makes his way safely to shore before paddling in himself.

It's a beautiful story of men looking out for boys, and helping them as they push their limits, but it's also a vivid image of what I hope to do as a bivocational pastor. The way Tom met my son in the surf, and watched over him, is a picture of how God's mission can take place in our workplaces and communities. We come alongside people in genuine relationships, we listen, and offer gentle guidance to the safe place – the relationship with the Creator that offers meaning and purpose to everything we do.

In Acts 8 there is a story of the apostle Phillip who is acutely attuned to the Spirit of God. The Spirit speaks to him and points him in the direction of an Ethiopian traveller, who is riding in a chariot and reading the book of Isaiah.

"Go and stay near."

It's not a complicated instruction. But proximity is the basis for all mission.

From there Phillip enquires as to what the Ethiopian is reading. The man explains that he is reading prophet Isaiah's words, but he is unable to make sense of them. Phillip is *near* and he is *listening*. He hasn't come to

EPILOGUE

sell the Ethiopian a 'salvation package'. But he has seen him searching and bewildered. He has observed his need for someone to guide him.

Phillip begins with the Ethiopian's questions, and then points him to Jesus as the source of life. A few minutes later the Ethiopian asks if he can be baptised in a river by the side of the road, and Phillip leads him in this affirmation of his new found faith.

It's a unique story of genuine human connection inspired by the Spirit of God. These simple actions are a template for us as we serve as bivocational missionaries:

- being present and available in the world;
- tuned to the Spirit and willing to respond;
- drawing near and listening;
- allowing people's questions to shape the conversation; and
- pointing them to Jesus.

I am grateful for Tom – grateful that he saw the young man flexing his muscles, who also needed an older head to guide him. In a similar vein, I hope to be a 'Tom' for those who are finding their way spiritually – a distinct and recognisable presence in our local area, so I am known as 'that guy', the irrigation repairer who is also a pastor. I want to listen to the people I work amongst. I want to be available with time to pause and engage. I want to have easy conversations with those asking questions. I want to be able to guide them to the path that leads to life and wholeness. Ultimately, I hope to introduce them to Jesus and his way, a decision that captured my own heart and imagination as a teenager and that still remains the deep core of my being today.

www.ingramcontent.com/pod-product-compliance
Lightning Source LLC
Chambersburg PA
CBHW060507090426
42735CB00011B/2138